The Films *of*
KIRK DOUGLAS

The Films *of*
KIRK DOUGLAS

by TONY THOMAS

with an introduction by
VINCENTE MINNELLI

THE CITADEL PRESS   Secaucus, New Jersey

First edition
Copyright © 1972 by Tony Thomas
All rights reserved
Published by Citadel Press, Inc.
A subsidiary of Lyle Stuart, Inc.
120 Enterprise Ave., Secaucus, N. J. 07094
In Canada: George J. McLeod Limited
73 Bathurst St., Toronto 2B, Ontario
Manufactured in the United States of America by
Halliday Lithograph Corp., West Hanover, Mass.
Designed by William Meinhardt
Library of Congress catalog card number: 72-85524
ISBN 0-8065-0297-5

The Bad and the Beautiful

Introduction *by Vincente Minnelli*

Working with Kirk Douglas in the three films we made together was for me the most rewarding and stimulating collaboration within my memory.

Lust for Life was the second of our pictures. My mind goes back to that especially because Vincent Van Gogh was one of the most controversial, contradictory and complex of men. A terrible and maddened genius, often sublime, sometimes grotesque. Fortunately, he left behind some five volumes of letters to his brother Theo, in which he discusses with great emotion his way of life at the moment, his views on paintings and other painters, and an enormous variety of subjects. But, the letters are maddening because he will argue with passion and conviction the affirmative of an idea, and then, often in the same letter, turn around and just as convincingly take the negative point of view.

One comes away with one's own conviction of how he would have behaved under certain conditions. It is any man's guess, and that is what makes the analysis so challenging. There may be many ways of conceiving the subject, and many of them can be right.

That is the extraordinary thing about our relationship on the picture, that we so often agreed and saw it the same way.

We started in France. I had been on another picture, and the day after finishing I flew to Arles in Southern France where they had been keeping a wheat field alive chemically for me to stage the suicide of Van Gogh. He was painting his last picture "Wheatfield with Crows" when he had his last attack and shot himself.

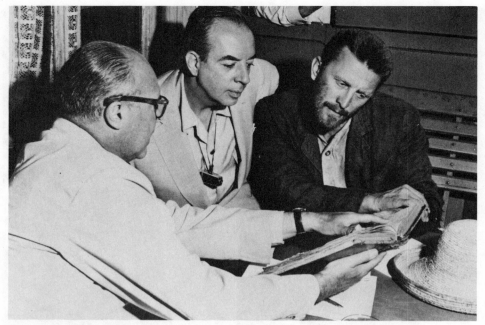

With director Vincente Minnelli (center) and producer
John Houseman on the set of *Lust for Life*

I had very little time to work with the producer and author, except on the
more broad aspects of the story, and had to make up for it now as we started the
shooting in Arles. "The Yellow House" had to be rebuilt on the original site
because it had been bombed out during the war, I was embarrassed to learn, by
the Americans.

Most of our shooting was done in Europe in the actual places where Van Gogh
had lived and worked during his tempestuous life. Arles, St. Rémy (the actual
asylum where he was incarcerated), the Borinage district in Belgium where he was
assigned as lay minister to the coal miners, the Dutch countryside, his father's
house, and the tiny church where his father was minister. Aubers, about twenty
miles outside of Paris (where he had gone to be treated by Dr. Gachet), in the inn
where he had died across from the Marie, which he painted. Also, Amsterdam,
where, besides our location shooting, we also shot in the studio Van Gogh painting
"The Potato Eaters" and "The Weaver" series, so it was necessary to redramatize
many of the scenes and incorporate new ones as these locations gave us a whole
different vision of the events.

Fortunately, the producer of the picture, John Houseman, was with us at all
times. He is also a writer of great imagination and great taste, and it was here
that Kirk proved an enormous contributing ally. Many of the touches in the film
were based on his ideas.

There is no more exciting thing for a director than the search with an actor
for the meaning of an illusive and challenging character. Kirk is blessed with tireless
energy, a willingness to try anything, and a complete disregard as to how he looks.
He could not care less about being the handsome hero. His enthusiasm and devotion
to the project is contagious and transmits itself to the crew, the cast, and everyone
connected with the picture.

Also, Van Gogh was a painter and painters have usually been notoriously
unconvincing on the screen. Together we studied the paintings and drawings in the
books and museums and analyzed the way Van Gogh must have painted, passion-

Two Weeks in Another Town

ately and brutally, with every nerve alive in his body and with the same ferocious energy with which he gave his friendship and his love and the way he met every happening in his short and tragic life.

Aside from his astonishing likeness to Van Gogh (he is depicted in various scenes with some of Vincent's many self-portraits), Kirk Douglas achieved a moving and memorable portrait of the artist—a man of massive creative power, triggered by severe emotional stress, the fear and horror of madness. In my opinion, Kirk should have won the Academy Award for which he was nominated.

So here's to Kirk, with affection, admiration, and amazement.

Acknowledgments

Books of this nature always require an author to seek help from others. In this particular enterprise I am grateful for the assistance of Mildred Simpson and her staff at the library of The Academy of Motion Picture Arts and Sciences in Los Angeles, and to Gerald Pratley and his staff at the Ontario Film Institute in Toronto. Thanks are also due Warren J. Cowan, Joan Eisleben, John Lebold, Gunnard Nelson, Richard Brooke, David Beard of Cinebooks (Toronto), Paula Klaw of *Movie Star News* (New York), Oliver Dernberger at Cherokee Books (Hollywood) and two Burbank friends—Ben Hartigan at the Disney Studio and Bill Latham at Warners. Lastly—and most obviously—I am grateful to Mr. and Mrs. Kirk Douglas.

Contents

Kirk Douglas at the age of fourteen

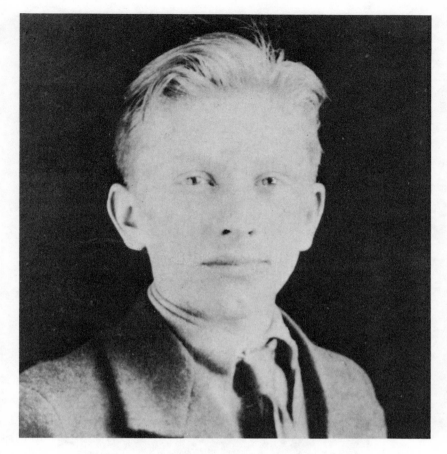

KIRK DOUGLAS:
The Man Behind the Actor

"The one thing in my life that I always knew, that was always constant, was that I wanted to be an actor. That in itself is an asset. I think half the success in life comes from first finding out what you really want to do. And then going ahead and doing it."

Robert Browning's belief that a man's reach should exceed his grasp is gospel with Kirk Douglas. The image is much the man. The qualities of intensity and forcefulness that have marked his performances as an actor have also accounted for his course in life. As Douglas knows full well, success as an actor comes only with determination and application: "You must know how to function and how to maintain yourself, and you must have a love of what you do. But an actor also needs great good luck. I have had that luck."

Kirk Douglas was born Issur Danielovitch, on December 9, 1916, in Amsterdam, New York. Both parents were Russian Jewish peasants from a village south of Moscow and they emigrated to the United States in 1910. They were impoverished and barely literate, and as Douglas recalls, "My mother once told me she literally expected to find gold bricks in the streets in America. These were the kinds

Douglas in 1939—his college grad-
uation picture

of myth that they grew up on, but later she said she'd found something more
valuable—the idea of a country where her son was able to work his way through
college, get a degree, and pursue the work he'd selected to do."

Douglas' life story is classically American, in the Horatio Alger sense. It is,
quite absolutely, a rags to riches story, and Douglas has frequently said it will
never serve as the plot for a film or a novel. "It's too typical, almost corny. You
can almost hear the violins in the background in this tale of a lad from the bottom
rungs of society climbing his way to the top of the ladder." It also happens to be
true. Douglas recalls his father, Herschel Danielovitch, as a personable and physically powerful man but totally unskilled and confused in his efforts to make a living.
He had a horse and wagon and plied the streets of Amsterdam as a peddler of food
and wood, and sometimes as a junk collector, but the income was not enough to
raise his family of six daughters and one son. Says Douglas, without humor, "Unless
you've been hungry-poor, you don't know what poor means."

Amsterdam, a town in New York's Mohawk Valley and about thirty miles
from Albany, was largely a one-industry town—rugs and carpets—with most of the
business handled by two companies, Mohawk Mills and Sanford Mills. Recalls
Douglas, "As a boy I sold pop and candy to the mill workers, to make enough
money to buy milk at seven cents a quart and bread at five cents a loaf. Sometimes
I made enough to buy a couple of boxes of corn flakes and two quarts of milk.
When that happened, the family had corn flakes and milk for dessert that night.

Kirk Douglas—then known as Isa-
dore Demsky—playing in a St.
Lawrence University production of
Death Takes a Holiday, in 1938

Whatever we had to eat, we ate every scrap. That habit has lasted all my life.
I seldom leave anything on my plate."

Kirk Douglas, known as Issy to his family and friends in his early days,
claims to have had more than forty jobs, mostly menial, prior to his becoming an
actor. While he was in school he delivered newspapers, both the early morning
and the evening editions. He does not look back on these experiences with the
warm nostalgia with which most people tend to color their recollections. Neither
does he look back fondly on being the only boy in a family of six sisters and a bread
winner at so early an age, "We laugh at it now but it was terrible. I hated being
the only male in a house full of women, I was dying to get out. In a sense, it lit a
fire under me. It's said that an actor is the kind of actor he is because of his
childhood and his life experiences, and that it's only possible to gauge his strength
and his weaknesses in view of that background. I think this is certainly true in
my own case."

It is not surprising that many actors come from traumatic backgrounds. The
sensitive, imaginative child tends to retreat into the fantasy of his own mind, and
the shy child sometimes overcomes his shyness by play-acting. When these feelings
are matched with ambition—in Douglas' case it amounted to an almost desperate
drive to escape—the result is often a powerful actor. "The first time the acting urge
manifested itself in me was when I was in the first grade at school. There was an
entertainment program involving children from kindergarten and the first grades,
and I recited a poem about the red robin of spring. When I was through, everybody
applauded—and when I heard that sound, an actor was born. That's the first remem-
brance I have of communicating, and communicate is what an actor does."

At Amsterdam's Wilbur Lynch High School, Douglas had the fortune to come
under the guidance of a teacher named Louise Livingston, who spotted his ability
and nurtured it. She introduced him to theatrical literature, and in time he was
appearing in school plays, entering oratorical contests and competing on debating

teams. At the age of thirteen, and still in school, Douglas took a job as a store clerk with the Goldmeer Wholesale Company, working evenings and Saturdays. When Sanford Mills put up money to buy a medal for the Amsterdam boy or girl who excelled in public speaking or in a ten-minute dramatic recitation, Douglas was the town's most eager contestant. He won by reciting *Across the Border,* a poem about a wounded soldier whose mind flitted back and forth between life and death. He was also asked by his employer to recite the poem for the Goldmeer salesmen, something he regards as one of his tougher performances.

The idea of college was in Douglas' mind from his earliest years, and in this ambition he was constantly encouraged by his mother. He graduated from school when he was seventeen and went to work as a clerk at Lurie's Department Store. He was still having to take home most of his earnings, since three of his sisters were younger than himself and by this time his father had left the family. At the end of a year Douglas had managed to save a total of $163. It was not enough to pay his way through college, but he decided to ask St. Lawrence University at Canton, New York, to take him anyway. He hitch-hiked to Canton, completing the last leg of the trip perched on top of a truck carrying a load of fertilizer. "I hadn't written to say I was coming, I hadn't even sent in an application. All I had were my high school credentials and $163, and an odor of fertilizer. Aware of my aroma and a bit defiant because of it, I went to see the Dean. I explained my predicament. He eyed me peculiarly, looked over my papers, and then told me he was willing

With son Michael during filming of *The Big Sky* in 1952

With father, mother and sisters

to take a chance. I arranged for a loan from the college and took a part-time job as a gardener at thirty cents an hour. I eventually lost this and then took to being a janitor."

Douglas worked exceedingly hard in his four years (1935 to 1939) at St. Lawrence. In addition to scholastic studies and sports activities, plus his side career as a laborer, he entered theatrical and debating groups. He became president of the student body and later president of The Mummers, the college dramatic group. He also excelled as a wrestler, ending up his final year as the undefeated champion of St. Lawrence and winner of the Intercollegiate Wrestling Championship. Always in need of money, Douglas put this ability to work. "One summer I made a few dollars wrestling with a carnival. We had an act in which I was the young man in the audience who stepped up to challenge the champ. There's where I got some of my best dramatic training."

Kirk Douglas' years at St. Lawrence were a triumph of will over lack of means. With no money he was unable to live in the college dormitory, so he bunked in the janitor's quarters. In the college cafeteria he ate with the aid of friends, each giving him a little from their own tray. He managed to attend college dances by checking the sick list to see who was incapacitated, and if no fellow student was ill he would pick upon a campus hypochondriac and talk him into a trip to the infirmary. Thus, with a second-hand ticket and a tuxedo borrowed from anyone who could be talked into lending it, Douglas leavened his workload with a little relaxation. In spite of all these difficulties, possibly because of them, he graduated from St. Lawrence with a bachelor of arts degree.

The next plateau in the Douglas career was the American Academy of Dramatic Arts in New York City. He had his sights set on this fortress and again he was not about to be deterred by lack of funds. The secretary of the Academy explained to the applicant that they had no scholarships, but Douglas was adamant in his determination to get in. He was given an audition, the persuasiveness of which caused the Academy to make an exception and create a special scholarship.

Douglas in Hollywood in late 1947, with his first wife, Diana, and his sons Michael, then three, and baby Joel

Douglas got himself a small room at a settlement house in Greenwich Village and found a string of odd jobs on the side. In his first year at the Academy he paid for his room and meals at the settlement house by teaching dramatics to house children in the evenings. His main job during his second year was as a waiter at a Schrafft's restaurant. In the summers he worked in summer stock theatres and earned his first money as an actor. It was during a summer stock season that he decided upon his professional name. He possibly chose Douglas because of the Douglas Fairbanks, Sr., image, and Kirk simply because it sounded "snazzy." He shrewdly reasoned that the name Danielovitch was not likely to help his career, and that Kirk Douglas would.

Shortly after he graduated from the Academy, Douglas went to see producer Guthrie McClintic. "He asked me if I could sing and I said I could but not well. He then asked if I could sing loud. Of course I could. He handed me a piece of paper and told me to learn the tune written on it—'Yankee Doodle.' I thought of my four years of college, two years at the Academy and a couple of seasons of summer stock. I had studied Shakespeare, the Greek tragedies, the French comedies, and here I was being asked to yearn 'Yankee Doodle.' However, it worked out well for me. I made my Broadway debut as a singing telegraph boy in *Spring Again,* delivering my musical telegram at the end of the second act."

The burgeoning young Douglas at St. Lawrence University: president of the student body, amateur actor, prize-winning debator, champion wrestler, and part-time janitor

Douglas' second Broadway show was Katharine Cornell's production of *The Three Sisters,* but in this he didn't get to appear on stage. He was an offstage echo. But it at least put him in good company. On Thanksgiving Day, 1941, Douglas was invited to attend a Cornell supper party, a startling contrast to the situation a year previously when he lined up at a Greenwich Village mission to get a free Thanksgiving dinner. This exposure to the world of high-class theatre was soon interrupted by a letter from Uncle Sam and a call to the colors. Douglas attended the midshipman school at Notre Dame University and was graduated as a naval ensign. He was assigned as a communications officer to Anti-submarine Unit 1139 in the Pacific. Douglas spent most of 1942 and 1943 on a small patrol craft. He was injured in an encounter with a Japanese submarine when a depth charge, set to explode in shallow water, went off (almost immediately after being discharged). Douglas suffered internal injuries, which was later complicated by amoebic dysentery. He spent five months at the Balboa Hospital at the San Diego Naval Station and was given a medical discharge in 1944.

When Kirk Douglas returned to resume his career in New York, he also returned to a wife. He had met Bermuda-born Diana Dill while they were both students at the American Academy of Dramatic Arts, and they married on November 2, 1943. Their son Michael was born September 25, 1944, and another son, Joel, was born to them on January 23, 1947. Douglas and his wife separated in 1949 and divorced two years later, stating their differences as stemming from career conflicts. The separation appears to have been fairly amicable and the two have since worked together professionally. Diana Douglas appeared with her ex-husband in *The Indian Fighter* in 1955, by which time he was married to Belgian-born Anne Buydens. Says Anne Douglas, "It's rather typical of Kirk that he would hire Diana in his first production. He has a sense of loyalty and responsibility to

Kirk Douglas is central in this squad of St. Lawrence University sportsmen

his family that borders on a guilt complex. You don't have to be a psychiatrist to realize this is a compensation for his father's lack of loyalty and responsibility. Kirk is, first and foremost, *a family man."* From his second marriage Douglas has two other sons, Peter, born November 23, 1955, and Eric, born June 21, 1958.

Douglas' first break in the acting profession came soon after returning to New York, when he took over the role played by Richard Widmark in *Kiss and Tell.* This lead to other offers; he played in *Trio,* and in *Star in the Window,* and received good notices for his playing of a sergeant from Oregon in *Alice in Arms.* He also worked as an actor in radio, then an extensive and flourishing field for actors, appearing in many network soap operas. He looks back on this experience as being particularly valuable and regrets that the same avenue is not open to actors today. Acting has much to do with the use of the voice, and the decline in the standards of diction and elocution may have something to do with the disappearance of radio as an outlet for drama.

It was Lauren Bacall who brought Douglas to the attention of Hollywood. She had been a classmate with him at the Academy and believed him to be a man with the special kind of appeal an actor needs to register on film. She persuaded Hal B. Wallis in this regard and, on his next trip to New York, Wallis went to see Douglas who was then rehearsing a play called *The Wind Is Ninety,* starring Wendell Corey, Bert Lytell, and Blanche Yurka. Recalls Douglas, "Wallis told me he'd like to do a screen test, and this startled me because I had never thought of working in the movies. My dream had always been to be a star on Broadway. Now, with opportunity knocking on the door like a woodpecker, I was scared. I told him I was sorry but that I wanted to stick with the play." *The Wind Is Ninety* was a major step forward in the Douglas career. This was June of 1945, and in his review for the *New York Herald Tribune,* Howard Barnes commented on Douglas: "Though he plays the impossible role of the Unknown Soldier, he plays it with a jaunty grace that endows it with dignity and feeling."

With the closing of *The Wind Is Ninety,* Douglas found himself with no follow-up job and short on cash. He reconsidered the Wallis offer and went to Paramount's New York office to get in touch with the producer. Wallis was as good as his word, he arranged for Douglas to be sent to the studio in Hollywood, where he was tested and soon given a lead role in *The Strange Loves of Martha Ivers,* opposite Barbara Stanwyck. After finishing the picture he returned to New York to appear in the Sam and Bella Spevak play *Woman Bites Dog.* The play had only a short run. Again there were no immediate offers for other plays and Douglas, now a married man with a son, began to think seriously about Hollywood. The reviews of *The Strange Love of Martha Ivers,* and the public response to it, made it obvious that Douglas was a natural film actor. His style and his personality came across on the screen, something that does not always happen, even with the finest actors. Douglas had, and has, a distinctly individual manner. He radiates a certain inexplicable quality, and it is this, as much as talent, that accounts for his success in films. He also came along at a time when styles in movie heroes were beginning to change—the storybook type of leading man began to wane after the Second World War and be replaced by a harder, more realistic working-man hero. In time it came to be more of an antihero than a hero, and Kirk Douglas' forceful, combative image has exemplified this trend. He states the case frankly: "I've made a career, in a sense, of playing sons-of-bitches, but I've always tried to show how a man got that way. The guy might not be any good but you must understand him. Often, in my films, he's a rebel against society, and most of us would like to say, 'To hell with society.' "

The image of Douglas as a tough guy did not jell until he did *Champion,* his eighth picture. Before that he had played weaklings and softies. It has been observed that Douglas' own personality underwent a change with the success of *Champion.* He had been described previously as somewhat shy and retiring in his demeanor but that description has seldom been used since then. Douglas says he quickly realized that the meek do not inherit the Hollywood earth and that his career would have declined had he not come to grips with the system and dictate his own terms. In 1948 his agent had arranged for him to play in an MGM picture, *The Great Sinner,* at a fee of fifty thousand dollars, his biggest to that time. But Douglas decided to gamble on an interesting offer from the then almost unknown Stanley Kramer to make a low-budget film about a viciously ambitious and ruthless prize fighter. It was the turning point in his career.

While Kirk Douglas is not a card-playing, pool-table type of gambler, he has always been willing to gamble on himself. He has never allowed his film career to drift, or to be controlled by others. He broke his contract with Hal B. Wallis a year after arriving in Hollywood because he wanted to be able to choose his own material and dictate his own course, and he terminated a long contract with Warner Bros. for the same reason. Douglas has not signed any studio contracts since 1952 and it is remarkable that he has maintained stardom over a twenty-year period on his own terms, choosing his own subjects and founding his own company. Bryna Productions was formed in 1955. "I chose to give it my mother's name not just from sentiment but because she was the one who instilled in me this business of gambling on yourself. I once had to tell her, while I was at St. Lawrence, that I had lost some of my hard-earned savings in a card game. She said, 'You're a fool. Why bet money on cards? What do they know about you? What do they care? If you want to bet, bet on yourself.' I found the perfect place to take her advice was in making films."

Although his popularity in films has been consistent, Kirk Douglas has not always been popular with those who work with him and for him. He has the reputation of being a compulsively hard worker who expects others to exude the same fierce energy and effort. He is exacting and demanding and sometimes painfully direct in his dealings with people working on his projects. Douglas admits to this, "I'd often been told how tough I was but I didn't realize how true it was until I went to work for myself." Those who have taken a dislike to him regard Douglas as egocentric, aggressive, vain, stubborn, and unfeeling.

Douglas in 1937, when he was a
student at St. Lawrence University

These are, of course, the views of people living in a sensitive, furtive and highly strung artistic community. Nonetheless, Douglas concedes, "I don't think I'd ever win any popularity contests in Hollywood, but I don't think I want to. I'm outspoken, perhaps too much so, but I imagine it's my way of saying things rather than what I say that makes people mad. I've always insisted on voicing my suggestions with directors. The good ones have never objected. I find the secure person will listen to you and be open, but the insecure man is fighting for his own dominance, and he's afraid that accepting another person's point of view will weaken his."

When they were working together in 1951 making *Ace in the Hole,* Billy Wilder kidded Douglas about the actor's eagerness to play every good role available in the business. He told him, "Kirk, you remind me of the old Austrian story about the man who committed suicide because he couldn't dance at two weddings at the same time. Kirk, you're a ham."

Most directors have their Kirk Douglas stories, but possibly the best insight into the actor was given by Melville Shavelson in his book *How to Make a Jewish Movie,* published in 1971 by Prentice-Hall. The book deals, humorously and sometimes acidly, with the making of *Cast a Giant Shadow* in Israel in 1965. Shavelson produced and directed the film and also wrote its script. His problems in making this expensive, large-scale, and sadly unsuccessful picture were many and varied, and in signing Douglas, Shavelson realized he was not setting himself up to work with the most malleable of actors. Says Shavelson, "There's something in his combative nature that gives him an authenticity in violent situations beyond mere histrionics."

As soon as Douglas arrived in Israel—he had just finished shooting *The Heroes of Telemark* in Norway—he and Shavelson got together to discuss the new picture and the star's role in it:

It didn't take me long to discover what my main problem was going to be: Kirk Douglas was *intelligent*. When discussing a script with actors, I have always found it necessary to remember that they never read the other actors' lines, so their concept of the story is somewhat hazy. Kirk had not only read the lines of everyone in the picture, he had also read the stage directions. This is considered indecent. A writer, resigned to having every line of dialogue examined, twisted, and changed by every actor billed above the title, can at least be certain that nobody cares enough about the stage directions to change them. So this is where he does his real writing, the little nuances, the flights of genius, that he knows will remain there for him to read and reread after he has seen the picture and failed to recognize a word he can call his own.

Kirk, I was to discover, always read every word, discussed every word, always argued every scene, until he was convinced of the correctness. Furthermore, he would listen to *logic*. He could not be dismissed as a star who must have everything his own way, making it a waste of time. He listened, so it was necessary to fight every minute.

Considerable factors in Kirk Douglas' success as a film actor are his good health and his seemingly inexhaustible supply of vitality and energy—qualities every bit as essential as talent. "It takes a lot out of you to work in this business. Many people fall by the wayside because they don't have the energy to sustain their talent. You draw on your own elements—you are your own stock in trade. The drive that got me out of my hometown and through college is part of the makeup that I utilize in my work. It's a constant fight, and it's tough."

Douglas has excelled in roles that call for intensity, such as *Champion, Detective Story, Lust for Life,* and *The Arrangement,* but he has also given gentle, restrained performances in *The Glass Menagerie, Act of Love, Paths of Glory, Lonely Are the Brave,* and *Seven Days in May.* He has been particularly effective in parts dealing with hard, ruthless men, such as the reporter in *Ace in the Hole,* and the film producer in *The Bad and the Beautiful.* His own choice of favorites tend to match those of the public, although any discussion of his best film work quickly brings from him, perhaps a little defensively, the mentioning of *Spartacus* and *The Vikings.* About his professional image and the unavoidable business of type-casting, Douglas says, "The audience tends to keep an actor at a certain level, they accept an image and they interpret you in the way they see you. They identify with a personality, which is an advantage in terms of popularity but pigeon-holing and limiting in terms of choice of material."

While the life of a movie star, with its fame and wealth, appears highly enviable, Douglas points out that it has drawbacks, "Stardom in any field brings with it some loneliness and suspicion, and a feeling of difference and isolation. Most people in this business have few close friends because they protect themselves with an entourage. The sad part—the frightening part—is that when a lot

Kirk Douglas in the Navy in 1943, somewhere in the Pacific

of us reach the top, and we have contracts and agents and managers and publicists, and such trappings as mansions and swimming pools, we're scared to death. We're afraid the whole glittering blob of quicksilver will slip through our fingers."

The aura of intense self-confidence that appears to mark Kirk Douglas is, in his own view, something of a shield. "Acting is the most direct way of escaping reality, and in my case it was a means of escaping a drab and dismal background. I have a theory that most actors are shy. People always seem surprised when I say this, but one of the best ways to overcome shyness is to play different roles. Actors are also people who never quite grow up. In fact, they are people who retain certain amounts of childlike naïvete, as must all artists. That childlike quality makes you receptive and curious. If an actor becomes blasé, he won't be able to play this game of 'let's pretend.' He's lost if he says to himself, 'Look at me, a grown man, pretending to be a cowboy shooting it out with Burt Lancaster in the O.K. Corral. This is ridiculous.' If you can't pretend without being self-conscious, you cannot be an actor. It's a bit like retarded development, which might account for the shyness, and you must retain a certain kind of innocence to remain an actor, because if you become sophisticated you'll start saying 'how silly' to the things you are required to do. On the other hand, despite all the snide things people say about actors, it is a job that demands a fine use of the intellect."

The Douglas home in Beverly Hills is a far cry from the poverty of his early years. It also speaks for a man who has acquired culture and refinement. Douglas is an art collector; he has a number of pre-Columbian pieces, and paintings by modernists and impressionists, including works by Chagall, Rouault, Utrillo, Picasso, and Vlaminck. The absence of Van Gogh paintings is something of a family joke. Says Douglas, "I can't afford one. Besides, I'd have the feeling

I painted it myself." Also conspicuous in the Douglas home are many autographed photos of high-ranking politicians and members of royalty, but few of movie stars. Again, the autographs of aristocrats stand in sharp contrast to his origins.

Many of the photos, especially those of John F. Kennedy and Lyndon B. Johnson—Douglas is a Democrat—resulted from extensive foreign tours the actor has made on behalf of the United States State Department. In 1963, he toured various countries in South America as a kind of "goodwill ambassador without portfolio," and the following year he toured in the Far East. Early in 1965 Douglas visited various European countries, and later the same year the Middle East. In 1966, he appeared in six Iron Curtain countries: Poland, Roumania, Bulgaria, Hungary, Czechoslovakia, and Yugoslavia. Always in the company of his wife, Douglas met with heads of state and addressed educators and student bodies. "The object of all this was to promote a better understanding of America. I know it's considered corny to talk of patriotism, but I do feel I owe this country something. I especially enjoy setting up dialogues with foreign students, and if the world is to survive we shall all have to get out and get to know each other."

Kirk Douglas' wife, Anne, is a gracious and refined woman with a vast fund of patience. She describes life with Douglas as "sitting in a beautiful garden right next to a volcano." They met when Douglas was working in Europe early in 1953 on *Act of Love,* for which film she was hired as a publicist. She is convinced that one of the main reasons for her success as Mrs. Kirk Douglas is the fact that she is not an actress, although she does understand the film business and its people. She is noted in Beverly Hills for her elegance of dress, and is consistently on the fashion lists as a best-dressed woman, and for her quiet, humorous temperament, which acts as a balance to the volatile personality of her husband. At their marriage ceremony in Las Vegas, Nevada, on May 29, 1954, the justice of the peace was a man with a slow Texas drawl. Barely able to understand what he was saying (her own language is French, and she was then not fluent in English), she tried to repeat the phrases of the marriage vows as chanted by the JP. Douglas

Douglas fooling around with Walt Disney on a Jamaican beach in 1954, while making *20,000 Leagues Under the Sea*

and the witnesses were surprised to hear his bride promise to "take this man for my awful wedded husband." He still thinks it was a Freudian slip.

Anne Douglas gives this impression of her husband: "He is a man with an enormous amount of heart and sensitivity, but he is also a man violently given to outbursts of feeling. He may be one of the most intensely active men alive. Kirk will get home from work in the afternoon, change clothes, go for a swim, play some tennis change his clothes make sixteen telephone calls, read a script, take me for a walk, make sixteen more telephone calls, gobble his dinner, run a movie on our living-room projector, read the newspaper and the trade papers, and finally crash into bed. Does he go to sleep? Yes, he goes to sleep instantly, but an hour later he wakes up with an idea, rushes to write it down, then wakes me up and insists on telling me about it. But I am not complaining—I love this wild man. He is very possessive, and thank goodness the possessiveness is all about his family. He truly is a man who loves to come home—and he *expects* us to be here."

According to his wife, Douglas is an actor who brings his work home with him. She says, "When he was doing *Lust for Life,* he came home in that red beard of Van Gogh's, wearing those big boots, stomping around the house—it was frightening. When he was playing *Spartacus,* I felt as if I were in every battle scene. This is fascinating to watch, this creative process, but sometimes it can be exhausting. It's difficult to say what causes Kirk to be the way he is. Part of his tension must come from his concern with his career. For a film actor it is not just the way he looks and learns and plays his part, it is a matter of planning his whole life. But he's not just an actor. Since 1955 he's also been a producer. He has to be involved with every infinitesimal detail. When he is in Hollywood he usually gets up between 5:30 and 7 A.M., and he is at the studio two hours later. By then he has seen three or four people, called New York or London or Paris a few times, and also found time to eat a good breakfast. He is a hearty eater, but he does not have to watch his diet too carefully because he paces off the poundage. He weighs around 170 pounds. This is what Americans call his 'fighting weight'— except that for Kirk any weight is his fighting weight."

Asked if she has arrived at any understanding of Douglas' enormous vitality and his incessant driving force, Anne Douglas opines: "I think it must be the life he had as a boy. To hear Kirk tell it, he was the poorest, most miserable child that ever lived. I think it would annihilate him to meet someone who was poorer than he says he was, he wouldn't be able to believe it. He was reared by his mother and his sisters and as a schoolboy he had to work to help support the family. I think part of Kirk's life has been a monstrous effort to prove himself and gain recognition in the eyes of his father. The old man is dead now—he died in 1954—but the pattern was set early, and not even four years of psychoanalysis could alter the drives that began as a desire to prove himself."

Kirk Douglas is serious about his work but less so about himself. He takes a good deal of ribbing from his sons about his tales of poverty as a child and how hard he worked. He also enjoys the humor in the many comic impersonations given of him, especially those of Frank Gorshin. Says Douglas, "Actually these mimics do us a service. They exaggerate the best and the worst things about your acting, and you should be wise enough to learn something from that. In my case they always pick on my intensity. This is one of my strengths but it is also a weakness—I try to look at my work with a critical eye and I sometimes find, shall we say, an over-abundance of intensity? Sometimes these impersonations intrigue me and I try to copy them. Then I'll come on heavy as Kirk Douglas around the house, and the boys will kid me 'Gorshin does it better.' "

Douglas has not encouraged any of his sons to enter the entertainment business, but the eldest, Michael, is now well established as a film actor. "I have no particular feelings about my sons choosing films as a profession. I only watch, as any father should, to see whether they select the métier which is best for them. And with all of them I've insisted on education. The basis of education is to enable you to think for yourself. All that I ask of my sons is that they function. I would never permit them to vegetate, as too many of their generation do. I don't care what they *do,* as long as they are doing something. It's a precious thing to retain the individuality of a child, and try to help that child develop his own personality and way of life so that he doesn't have the shadow of his parents smothering him. I insist on education."

Kirk Douglas does not glorify the fact that he rose from the lower strata of society and that he worked his way through college. "There's a tendency to romanticize these things. I'm against a boy having to work his way through school the way I did. It's a waste of precious time for him to be working part time as a waiter or a gardener. All his time should be spent working on his studies and on sports, and some real fun and relaxation. I find my own sons much more informed than I was at their age, much more aware of life. It took me years to concentrate on being a human being—I was too busy scrounging for money and food, and struggling to better myself. I don't recommend that route. This is partly what Kazan was writing about in *The Arrangement.* The film was a failure, but I still feel the concept, and much of the effort put into it, was magnificent. I knew exactly what Kazan had in mind with his hero Eddie. Here was a middle-aged man who one day looked in the mirror and didn't like what he saw—the phony

BETWEEN SCENES . . . Kirk Douglas perches on the camera platform in Rome while watching filming of a scene for *Two Weeks in Another Town*

Michael Douglas, and father

Madison Avenue image of the affluent advertising executive. So he tried to turn hippie—twenty years too late, and with disastrous results. A lot of my playing of Eddie was autobiographical. I'm not discontented with my own lot in life, I've done well, but I know that kind of man and how he got that way, and I can understand why the younger generation look at us with disdain."

Commenting further on the attitudes and problems of his sons' generation, Douglas says: "The current trends don't surprise me at all. The changes that are taking place are ones which the youth of today have perpetrated. There's always danger in revolution, but I think it's good that they are questioning the 'establishment.' I only hope they are fully aware that the pendulum can swing the other way. It's much easier to criticize a situation than to correct it. But I think it's healthy that our children have questioned the moral values of the adult world, although I don't see too much difference now from the days when my generation was considered rebellious. As an interested onlooker I think it boils down to a good imagination on the child's part and a good memory on the parent's—a child can only try to imagine what it must be like to be a parent, and a parent ought to be able to remember what it's like to be a child."

As he appeared in Broadway play *One Flew Over the Cuckoo's Nest*

After a quarter of a century as a Hollywood star, Kirk Douglas is still intent on averaging two films a year, mostly films on which he has a hand in the production and frequently on which he has been responsible for raising the financing. The slump in film production in California has not affected his career because he has not been content to rely upon the Hollywood scene. When funding has not been forthcoming locally, Douglas has been enterprising enough to seek it elsewhere, particularly in Europe. He looks upon the decline of Hollywood in the late 1960's as the result of antiquated production and distribution methods. He sees the decline as temporary, and the future of film as burgeoning.

That Kirk Douglas will continue to be a force in film making seems more than likely. Director Melville Shavelson makes this comment on the Douglas drive: "The hungry, relentless battler of *Champion* is still fighting, several million dollars later, slugging his way toward some invisible championship that continues, apparently, to elude him." Douglas will also continue as an actor-producer because of his tough attitude toward the business involved in making films. He looks at *Lonely Are the Brave,* one of his favorite films and one regarded with respect by critics and film students, as something of a failure, "This has much to do with the way the studio presented and distributed it. They looked upon it as being not very commercial, and the way they handled it made it exactly that. If a movie doesn't make money, you have failed. I realize that makes me sound hard-nosed but my point is this: it isn't just a case of making money. It's the fact that the lack of revenue means not enough people have seen that picture, and that's what you make them for, to be seen."

Kirk Douglas concedes he is a man with vanity, "I don't think I'd be much of an actor without vanity. And I'm not interested in being a 'modest actor.' The last time I heard a star described that way, I was reminded of the classic retort, 'He has a lot to be modest about.' I look at my work and I see performances I don't like and some that I do. I was happy that I was nominated for Oscars for *Champion, The Bad and the Beautiful,* and *Lust for Life,* and I was terribly disappointed not to win, especially for *Lust for Life,* I really thought I had a chance with that one. I was also hurt about *Detective Story,* I thought that performance was Oscar caliber but I didn't even get nominated. However, I don't want to appear ungrateful. I've been very lucky. Few people manage to do what they want in life. I have."

Although he set out with the idea of being a stage actor, Kirk Douglas is pleased that his career steered him into the film world, "I'm very happy with this industry. I have a high opinion of films, possibly higher than that of most people. To me it is the most important art form—it *is* an art, and it includes all the elements of the modern age. And the most important thing about film, in my opinion, is its entertainment value. You can make a statement, you can say something, but it must be entertaining. I think there is great therapeutic value in enabling people to watch a movie for a couple of hours and lose themselves in it. This was most vividly pointed out to me in Yugoslavia by Marshall Tito. I was amazed to find him to be a great movie fan. He sees a film almost every night, and he seemed to know all of mine. I asked him why he loved pictures so much and he said, 'I find them relaxing. If I watch you in *The Vikings,* I can forget my problems for a little while.' I think that's as good a reason for making movies as I can find. Very often we get pretentious about films. I've attempted to make statements in films, but I have to constantly remind myself that it is my business to tell a story. If you have a message it must be a by-product. A film can be revealing about life and people, it can be informative and enlightening, but it must first be interesting and amusing and exciting. In short, it must be entertaining."

Three producers and directors

comment on KIRK DOUGLAS

WILLIAM WYLER:

My association with Kirk Douglas was limited to a single picture, *Detective Story,* but it was the best star-director relationship I ever had. We made the film in five weeks, the shortest schedule I ever had on a major motion picture, and it was thanks to Kirk and his professionalism that such a schedule was possible. He's a great fellow as an actor and as a man.

HAL B. WALLIS:

Kirk Douglas has justifiably earned the status of a star. He also is one of the most interesting and creative people in the motion picture industry. In addition, Kirk was among the first actors who formed a successful independent production company which has made many highly successful films.

I recognized his potential as a motion picture star when I first saw him on Broadway in the stage play *The Wind Is Ninety*. I brought Kirk to Hollywood for a screen test, which convinced me to sign him to a long-term contract and to give him his opportunity in my production *The Strange Love of Martha Ivers,* opposite Barbara Stanwyck, which paved his way to stardom. Among his other critically acclaimed performances in my other films was his memorable role of Doc Holliday in *Gunfight at the O.K. Corral*.

STANLEY KRAMER:

We made a peculiar chemistry together. I chose him for *Champion*—he chose me—when both of us had other choices open, but not too many. He was a star. He acted like a star when he was nobody. Nothing daunted—to learn a language, to be a prize fighter, to juggle, to paint, to dance, to do *anything*. Dimple akimbo . . . he came at you, center stage, and there it was . . . talented, full of chutzpah—and class. In that early film, he screamed at the fight manager: "I can do it—I can do it!" He can. He can.

The Films *of*
KIRK DOUGLAS

With Barbara Stanwyck

The Strange Love
of Martha Ivers

1946 A Hal B. Wallis Production, *distributed by* Paramount. *Produced by* Hal B. Wallis. *Directed by* Lewis Milestone. *Written by* Robert Rossen, *based on a story by* Jack Patrick. *Photographed by* Victor Milner. *Edited by* Archie Marshek. *Art Directors:* Hans Dreir *and* John Meehan. *Musical score by* Miklos Rozsa. *Running time:* 117 minutes.

CAST: Barbara Stanwyck *(Martha Ivers)*, Van Heflin *(Sam Masterson)*, Lizabeth Scott *(Toni Marachek)*, Kirk Douglas *(Walter O'Neil)*, Judith Anderson *(Mrs. Ivers)*, Roman Bohnen *(Mr. O'Neil)*, Daryl Hickman *(Sam Masterson* [as a boy]), Janis Wilson *(Martha Ivers* [as a girl]), Ann Doran *(Secretary)*,

Frank Orth *(Hotel Clerk)*, James Flavin *(Detective No. 1)*, Mickey Kuhn *(Walter O'Neil* [as a boy]), Chester D. Brown *(Special Investigator)*.

The popular image of Kirk Douglas as a tough, forceful, tenacious man was not apparent in his first film. In *The Strange Love of Martha Ivers* Douglas appeared as a weakling, a man dominated by a vicious woman and made a criminal accomplice by her. Despite the softness and unpleasantness of the part, Douglas made the man sympathetic. He gave his weakling a little humor and warmth, and the suggestion that under other circumstances he might have been a good and decent man. It was a remarkably effective performance and it assured Douglas his future in films.

[33]

It was immediately apparent that Kirk Douglas, even though he may not have realized it himself, was a natural film actor. He had, and has, that strange, indefinable *something,* a presence that has a kind of invisible phosphorescence. If matched with ability, it is the quality that enables an actor to become a star.

The Strange Love of Martha Ivers is a black jigsaw of a story, full of nasty, ruthless people engaged in extortion and murder. The film is an unlikely melodrama, but it is made fascinating by the craftsmanship of its actors, by the script of Robert Rossen, the music of Miklos Rozsa, and the skillful direction of Lewis Milestone—all under the command of the shrewd Hal Wallis.

Barbara Stanwyck had played many a vixen before this film—her greedy, murderous wife in *Double Indemnity* being a prime example—but her Martha Ivers allowed for the sketching of an especially loathsome lady. As the wealthy and powerful ruler of Iverstown, Pennsylvania, one of those family towns so popular in American fiction, Martha sends an innocent man to the gallows to cover up her own accidental slaying of her aunt (Judith Anderson) who had found the thirteen-year-old Martha about to run

With Barbara Stanwyck

With Barbara Stanwyck and Van Heflin

With Barbara Stanwyck

away with a young lad named Sam Masterson (Darryl Hickman). The youth leaves Iverstown and eventually becomes a gambler, returning seventeen years later in the guise of Van Heflin. Heflin was himself, with this picture, returning to Hollywood after three years in the Air Force. It was a good role for him, and he quickly resumed his film career.

The strange love of the title is never quite clear. It can only refer to the love Stanwyck feels for Heflin when he returns to Iverstown, but it is a love more perverse than strange. Young Martha Ivers had assumed her boyfriend to be a witness to the killing of her aunt, whereas he had in fact not actually seen the crime. However, another youngster did see

With Van Heflin and Barbara
Stanwyck

On the set with Barbara Stanwyck

he has pieced the mystery together, Heflin, almost as unprincipled as the other characters in this story, is prepared to blackmail. Stanwyck then tries to rekindle their old love and Heflin falls for her. But he balks at the idea of the two of them teaming up to murder Douglas. Sensing disaster, the drunken district attorney spills the truth to Heflin and then falls down a flight of stairs and breaks his neck. Stanwyck chooses suicide rather than face trial and Heflin has little choice but to leave the wretched scene.

The Strange Love of Martha Ivers is an evil tale, but like so many other stories of wicked people in dreadful situations, it casts a spell. The film is dark and moody, and expertly made. Lewis Milestone, who won an Oscar for *All Quiet on the Western Front* (1930) and who directed a number of fine films about the Second World War, including *Edge of Darkness, North Star,* and *The Purple Heart,* was a master of realism. His was a fluid camera style, impersonal rather than personal, and in giving *The Strange Love of Martha Ivers* a realistic, matter-of-fact atmosphere, he gave chilling credence to an improbable picture.

Martha clobber her aunt with a heavy cane and it is this youngster who grows up to be the character played by Kirk Douglas. The young man's father, a rough workingman played by the memorable Roman Bohnen, engineers a marriage between his son and Martha and thus assures himself a soft touch for the remainder of his life. Once married, Douglas is appointed district attorney of Iverstown, although actually just another pawn in the life of the town whose economy is governed by Stanwyck. The marriage means nothing to her and she carries on various amorous affairs, while her husband drowns his sorrow in drink.

It is the return of Heflin to Iverstown that sets off the chain of events that results in the collapse of the Ivers family. He falls in love with a girl (Lizabeth Scott) who has recently been released from jail, and when she is picked up by the police and returned to jail Heflin visits the district attorney to effect her release. Stanwyck and Douglas think that Heflin has reappeared in Iverstown in order to blackmail them, and they devise maneuvers to ward him off, including having him beaten up. Only then are Heflin's doubts raised about the pair; he examines old newspapers and concludes that an innocent man was sent to the gallows on perjured evidence. Once

With Van Heflin

With Robert Mitchum

Out of the Past

1947   An RKO Radio Picture. *Produced by* Warren Duff. *Directed by* Jacques Tourneur. *Written by* Geoffrey Homes. *Photographed by* Nicholas Musuraca. *Edited by* Samuel E. Beetley. *Art Directors*, Albert S. D'Agostino *and* Jack Okey. *Musical score by* Roy Webb. *Running time:* 97 minutes.

CAST: Robert Mitchum *(Jeff)*, Jane Greer *(Kathie)*, Kirk Douglas *(Whit)*, Rhonda Fleming *(Meta Carson)*, Richard Webb *(Jim)*, Steve Brodie *(Fisher)*, Virginia Huston *(Ann)*, Paul Valentine *(Joe)*, Dickie Moore *(The Kid)*, Ken Miles *(Eels)*.

With Paul Valentine and Robert Mitchum

Jane Greer and Robert Mitchum

In his excellent survey of the work of American directors, *The American Cinema,* Andrew Sarris claims that *Out of the Past* remains the masterpiece of Jacques Tourneur: "a civilized treatment of an annihilating melodrama." Tourneur had directed in his native France before coming to Hollywood, where he began working in 1939. His style was generally gentle and he had a marked flair for the macabre, turning out such cult favorites as *Cat People* and *I Walked With a Zombie.* His direction of *Out of the Past* balances mood and action, and he unfolds a complicated plot with lucidity, without which the film would have been destructively confusing. Tourneur is especially good in developing the characterizations of his actors, and moving them through the story maze.

Out of the Past has Robert Mitchum as its central character, a retired private detective who now runs a gas station in a small town and looks forward to a future more peaceful and less sordid than his past. But his past will not let him rest. He is visited by a hoodlum in the employ of a big-league criminal (Kirk Douglas) and told to report for another job. Mitchum explains to his girl friend why he has no choice but to comply. In a lengthy flashback sequence Tourneur shows Mitchum being sent to trail beautiful villainess Jane Greer, who absconds with $40,000 after shooting her lover, Douglas. Finding her in Acapulco, Mitchum succumbs to her charms and settles down with her rather than turn her in. He learns the truth about her vicious character, becoming particularly disenchanted

With Paul Valentine and Robert Mitchum

Rhonda Fleming and Robert Mitchum

when required to dispose of the body of one of her victims.

It is then that Mitchum decides to retire from sleuthing and seek obscurity. The treacherous but charming Greer then works her way back into the affections of Douglas, who realizes he has something on Mitchum and will be able to summon him whenever the need arises. It arises when Douglas gets into trouble with income tax evasion, and he calls Mitchum to locate and steal incriminating records. The job is not as simple as stated and it involves double-crossing and murder, culminating in the death of almost the entire cast of the picture. Douglas and Greer end up as corpses, as they deserve, but the intrigue also costs the unlucky detective his life. To heighten the bitter injustice, his girl friend is allowed to assume that Mitchum was a mean and unworthy man, whereupon she takes up with another man. The moral is blunt and painful—"That's life."

Out of the Past is notable for excellent casting. Mitchum is perfect as the laconic, fatalistic investigator and Jane Greer has never done anything better than this portrait of a lovely, evil-hearted lady. Kirk Douglas consolidated his early claim to movie stardom with an unconventional characterization of a master crook. Douglas conveys the fanaticism of a dedicated criminal, glowing with a kind of low-keyed intensity, but the role is leavened with charm. This is a hood with refinement, and all the more frightening for it.

Adding to the quality of *Out of the Past* are its locations. Tourneur not only moves the story in terms of tempo but he moves it from Los Angeles to San Francisco to Nevada to Mexico. In the genre of crime-intrigue-suspense films, this is an item worth studying. The story is not great, but the style with which it is delivered is admirable.

With Jane Greer and Robert Mitchum

With Nancy Coleman and Katina Paxinou

Mourning Becomes Electra

1947   An RKO Radio Picture. *Produced, directed and written by* Dudley Nichols. *Based on the play by* Eugene O'Neill. *Photographed by* George Barnes. *Edited by* Roland Gross *and* Chandler House. *Art director,* Albert D'Agostino. *Musical score by* Richard Hageman. *Running time (first release):* 173 minutes.

CAST: Rosalind Russell *(Lavinia Mannon),* Michael Redgrave *(Orin Mannon),* Raymond Massey *(Ezra Mannon),* Katina Paxinou *(Christine Mannon),* Leo Genn *(Adam Brant),* Kirk Douglas *(Peter Niles),* Nancy Coleman *(Hazel Niles),* Henry Hull *(Seth Beckwith),* Sara Allgood *(Landlady),* Thurston Hall *(Dr. Blake),* Walter Baldwin *(Amos Ames),* Elizabeth Risdon *(Mrs. Hills),* Erskine Sanford *(Josiah Borden),* Jimmy Conlin *(Abner Small),* Lee Baker *(Rev. Hills),* Tito Verolo *(Joe Silva),* Emma Dunn *(Mrs. Borden),* Nora Cecil *(Louise Ames),* Marie Blake *(Minnie),* Clem Bevans *(Ira Mackel),* Jean Clarenden *(Eben Nobel).*

Dudley Nichols' screen version of Eugene O'Neill's *Mourning Becomes Electra* is, regrettably, a perfect example of the many differences in technique and impact between film and stage plays. What is acceptable in the one medium is not workable in the other. Nichols edited down the six hours of the O'Neill stage original to a three-hour framework and then, with admirable but unwise deference, attempted to film the work almost literally. The play had been considered for filming at previous times but always met with rejection. Backed with the approval of the playwright and the eager participation of Rosalind Russell and Raymond Massey, Nichols was able to raise the money for the project.

Presented by RKO Radio Pictures as a *prestige* item, possibly the only one in which that soon-to-be-defunct studio was ever involved, they soon found *Mourning Becomes Electra* to be a nonprofit enterprise. They first tried it as a road-show attraction, with an intermission, in eastern American cities, and then sent it to western bookings minus twenty-five of its original minutes. Critics were generally kind, but the public was largely unimpressed. RKO sliced another twenty minutes out of it for the general release, thereby adding confusion to its dullness.

With Rosalind Russell and Katina
Paxinou

With Michael Redgrave and
Rosalind Russell

The O'Neill play is a Greek tragedy set in the Massachusetts of 1865; it is, in fact, an adaptation of *Oresteia,* with the Electra of the Greek original becoming Lavinia Mannon, the daughter of a prominent patrician family. It is a relentless period drama of grim affairs, sombre in its settings and bitter in its moral tone. The performances are mostly verbal, and handled by Nichols with stage technique, the dialogue supplanting action.

The story concerns the hatred and spite within the Mannon family. It has moments of passion and eloquence, and its attraction, for those seriously interested in dramatic art, lies in the performances of Massey, Katina Paxinou, and Michael Redgrave, with Rosalind Russell good but somewhat beyond her depth. For Kirk Douglas it is a minor assignment, a fairly routine playing of a colorless part, but one for which the new Hollywood actor was quickly cast, having only just recently graduated from the boards of Broadway.

Unhappy though the results may have been, Nichols and his cast and crew deserve full marks for the courage of their convictions and for their admirable labors. Even had it been more vitally filmed, *Mourning Becomes Electra* could never have found a wide market, as Nichols and his backers must have known.

The fascination of *Mourning Becomes Electra,* in this or any presentation, lies in the performances of its actors, in their shadings of the long speeches, in the subtlety of cunning, calculated, diabolical battles of wits. The playing in Nichols' version is of a high order, with Katina Paxinou brilliant as the mother.

The Mannons are a family smitten with evil: the mother murders the father (Massey), and her lover (Leo Genn) is murdered by her children. It is Lavinia's jealousy of her mother that motivates the tragedies, jealousy bred by her inordinate devotion to her father and the discovery that the man she loves is her mother's lover. Lavinia incites her weakling brother (Redgrave) to murder, and drives her mother to suicide. Guilt complexes corrode the personalities and defy all hope of happiness. A young army officer (Douglas) falls in love with Lavinia but the affair is doomed.

At the end of the story, Lavinia becomes a recluse in the Mannon mansion, living out her life in loneliness and darkness. As stage drama *Mourning Becomes Electra* is raw, fundamental and compelling; this screen version is perhaps best described as an interesting and admirable failure.

With Nancy Coleman, Michael Redgrave and Katina Paxinou

I Walk Alone

1947 A Hal B. Wallis Production, *distributed by* Paramount. *Produced by* Hal B. Wallis. *Directed by* Byron Haskins. *Written by* Charles Schnee. *Adapted by* Robert Smith *and* John Bright *from the play Beggars Are Coming to Town by* Theodore Reeves. *Photographed by* Leo Tover. *Edited by* Arthur Schmidt. *Art directors,* Hans Dreir *and* Franz Bachelin. *Musical score by* Victor young. *Running time:* 98 minutes.

CAST: Burt Lancaster *(Frankie Madison),* Lizabeth Scott *(Kay Lawrence),* Kirk Douglas *(Noll Turner),* Wendell Corey *(Dave),* Kristine Miller *(Mrs. Richardson),* George Rigaud *(Maurice),* Marc Lawrence *(Nick Palestro),* Mike Mazurki *(Dan),* Mickey Knox *(Skinner),* Roger Neury *(Felix).*

I Walk Alone was the first pairing of Kirk Douglas and Burt Lancaster, and the fourth film in the career

of each actor, Lancaster having previously appeared in *The Killers, Desert Fury,* and *Brute Force.* Both Douglas and Lancaster, older by three years, came to Hollywood in 1946 from the New York stage, and both were signed to contracts by Hal B. Wallis. There are obvious similarities in style, but Douglas and Lancaster are also similar in being actor-producers largely responsible for choosing their own film projects.

Sheilah Graham devotes a chapter of her *Confessions of a Hollywood Columnist* to them and calls them "The Terrible-Tempered Twins." The chapter is generally unflattering but it accurately describes the two stars as tough-minded, hard-driving and shrewd movie makers. These characteristics showed up even during the making of *I Walk Alone,* with both Douglas and Lancaster arguing with Wallis over their roles and complaining that they were underpaid.

Douglas' contract with Wallis called for five films, but the discontented actor broke the contract after making this one, the second. Ten years later Douglas and Lancaster teamed up to star in another

With Burt Lancaster

Wallis film, *Gunfight at the O.K. Corral,* but with each actor getting a salary possibly equal to the entire budget of *I Walk Alone.*

Although expertly crafted, *I Walk Alone* is not an especially likable picture because its entire cast is composed of villainous characters, for whom it is difficult to feel much sympathy. This is a darkly shaded melodrama of a convict released after fourteen years in a penitentiary, having served a sentence that should have been shared with his partner. A flashback sequence shows Lancaster and Douglas as Prohibition-period rum-runners who have enjoyed some success with their racket but who, on one particular caper, are pounced upon by the police. The

With Burt Lancaster and Lizabeth Scott

With Wendell Corey and Burt
Lancaster

wily, treacherous Douglas manages to slip away and
Lancaster takes the rap.

With their ill-gotten gains, Douglas builds up an
underground business, of which the front is a swank,
expensive nightclub. When Lancaster returns to freedom he expects an equal partnership in the operation, which Douglas has no intention of giving him.
It takes Lancaster a long time to realize he is an
old-fashioned hood, unwanted by an ex-partner now
managing a corporation, divided into subsidiaries
and set up with elaborate bookkeeping methods.

Wendell Corey, as an intimidated accountant,

With Burt Lancaster and Lizabeth
Scott

On the set with Burt Lancaster

has to explain to Lancaster that he cannot legally lay claim to a business with bonds, holding companies and shrewd, albeit crooked, lawyers. When Lancaster then tries to bulldoze his way in, he gets badly beaten, including a savage roughing-up from Mike Mazurki.

The only sympathetic character in *I Walk Alone,* and then only by comparison, is Lizabeth Scott as the resident singer of the Regent Club and the girl-friend of Douglas. Scott, then at the top of her brief fling at stardom, appears to advantage singing a torch ballad, "Don't Call It Love." The slinky, husky-voiced blonde takes a shine to Lancaster and switches her affections to him, eventually helping him to dethrone Douglas. When he suspects Corey is also sympathetic to Lancaster and likely to reveal incriminating evidence, Douglas has him killed and manages to circumstantially point the blame at Lan-

caster. Lancaster eludes the police and he cunningly sets a trap for Douglas, in which the despicable crook reveals himself and admits his crimes.

Such is the moral tone of *I Walk Alone* that the Lancaster character becomes somehow admirable, and certainly sympathetic, even though the man is an ex-gangster presumably intent on resuming his career. The ending of the film allows us to assume that with the aid of Scott he will rehabilitate himself along straight lines, but it is a thin assumption.

For Kirk Douglas the film allowed the portrayal of an unusually amoral villain, a man with no re-deeming qualities, avaricious, cruel and heartless. Douglas carried off the nasty part with style but coming so soon after his similarly villainous image in *Out of the Past,* the ambitious actor was wise to look for different material.

The Walls of Jericho

1948 A 20th Century-Fox Film. *Produced by* Lamar Trotti. *Directed by* John M. Stahl. *Written by* Lamar Trotti, *based on the novel by* Paul Wellman. *Photographed by* Arthur Miller. *Edited by* James B. Clark. *Art directors,* Lyle Wheeler *and* Maurice Ransford. *Musical score by* Cyril Mockridge. *Running time:* 111 minutes.

CAST: Cornel Wilde *(Dave)*, Linda Darnell *(Algeria)*, Anne Baxter *(Julia)*, Kirk Douglas *(Tucker Wedge)*, Ann Dvorak *(Belle)*, Marjorie Rambeau *(Mrs. Dunham)*, Henry Hull *(Jefferson Norman)*, Colleen Townsend *(Marjorie Ransome)*, Barton MacLane *(Gotch McCurdy)*, Griff Barnett *(Judge Hutto)*, William Tracy *(Cully Caxton)*, Art Baker *(Peddigrew)*, Frank Ferguson *(Tom*

With Linda Darnell

Ransome), Ann Morrison *(Nellie)*, Hope Landis *(Mrs. Hutte)*, Helen Brown *(Mrs. Ransome)*, Norman Leavitt *(Andy Mc-Adam)*, Whitford Kane *(Judge Foster)*, J. Farrell MacDonald *(Bailiff)*, Dick Rich *(Mulliken)*, Will Wright *(Dr. Patterson)*.

The Walls of Jericho is not, at least in this telling, a biblical tale, although it has all the elements of one: love, hate, greed, envy, ambitiousness, lies, scandal, and murder. It is a solidly constructed soap opera, aimed at female audiences, with Cornel Wilde as an upright, victimized lawyer, vied for by three women. Kirk Douglas is here purely as a supporting player, the best friend of the hero, not much of a part but a welcome relief from playing sadistic villains.

The Jericho of the title is a small town on the plains of Kansas in 1908. Wilde is the county prosecutor, married to a dipsomaniac (Ann Dvorak), a woman below his station and spitefully aware of it. The wife (Linda Darnell) of his best friend makes overtures to him, but Wilde fends them off. Angered, she alienates the two old friends, and encourages her husband, a newspaper publisher, to disparage Wilde. The rift between Wilde and Douglas grows, and becomes a problem to the young lawyer in his ambitions to run for political office. His problems are complicated by the love of a beautiful girl (Anne Baxter) who has just graduated from law school. Wilde finds himself falling in love with her, as well

With Linda Darnell

as finding himself smeared as an immoralist by publisher Douglas, who is also running for political office, edged on by his beautiful but vicious wife.

As the passions and lies swirl around him, Wilde gives up his political plans, in addition to persuading

With Cornel Wilde and Linda Darnell

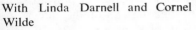
With Linda Darnell and Cornel Wilde

Baxter to leave town and live elsewhere. Meanwhile, Douglas wins his election and takes off for Washington, although his wife continues to spin her evil influence in Jericho. When a mutual friend is convicted of manslaughter, Wilde and Baxter are reunited as they both appear as defense counsel. The local newspaper comes out with a headline revealing that Wilde is being sued for divorce and that his fellow lawyer is the co-respondent. Dvorak, in a drunken rage cultivated by Darnell, shoots her husband.

As Wilde lies in the hospital, his life hanging in the balance, Baxter continues the courtroom battle and wins it. Later, a sober and contrite Dvorak confesses that she was driven to desperation by Darnell, at which Douglas declares that he too has had enough of all this nonsense, and that he is shedding his nasty wife. Baxter visits the hospital and tells Wilde of their victory, presumably a victory in more ways than one. Such is the stuff of *The Walls of Jericho*.

With Ann Dvorak, Cornel Wilde and Linda Darnell

With Laraine Day

My Dear Secretary

1948   A Harry M. Popkin—Leo C. Popkin Production. *Distributed by* United Artists. *Directed and written by* Charles Martin. *Photographed by* Joseph Biroc. *Edited by* Arthur H. Nadel. *Art director,* Rudi Feld. *Musical score by* Heinz Roemheld. *Running time:* 83 minutes.

CAST: Laraine Day *(Stephanie Gaylord),* Kirk Douglas *(Owen Waterbury),* Keenan Wynn *(Ronnie Hastings),* Helen Walker *(Elsie),* Rudy Vallee *(Charles Harris),* Florence Bates *(Mrs. Reeves),* Alan Mowbray *(Deveny),* Grady Sutton *(Scott),* Irene Ryan *(Mary),* Gale Robbins *(Dawn O'Malley),* Virginia Hewitt *(Felicia),* Abe Reynolds *(Taxi Driver),* Jody Gilbert *(Hilda Snee-*

bacher), Helene Stanley *(Miss Pidgeon),* Joe Kirk *(Process Server),* Russell Hicks *(Publisher),* Gertrude Astor *(Miss Gee),* Martin Lamont *(Male Secretary).*

My Dear Secretary is typical of the kind of films dramatic actors end up in when they are desperate to appear in comedies. All the good comedic pictures go to the established comedic players. Charlton Heston once said that scripts for light comedies came to him slightly soiled with the finger prints of Cary Grant. Whether the script of *My Dear Secretary* was read and turned down by other actors is hard to prove, but it was accepted by an eager Kirk Douglas, who by now wanted to display the lighter side of his acting ability. He had reason to be concerned with type-casting in somber pictures.

With Charles Halton

The plot is fragile and far from believable, and it is saved from total absurdity by its cast, especially its veteran character actors, such as Florence Bates as a landlady, Irene Ryan as a kitchen maid, and Keenan Wynn as a man-of-all-work roommate taken advantage of by Kirk Douglas. Douglas whizzes through the film as a successful novelist, a dashing fellow with a keen appetite for attractive women. How he manages to find time to write novels is a mystery known only to those who write scripts for films like this one. Douglas apparently invents his plots when not betting on races at Santa Anita, roulette gambling in Las Vegas, and making love in his plush bachelor pad.

The story recounts the amorous adventures of Douglas and Laraine Day, who gives up her job as secretary to book publisher Rudy Vallee to work in the same capacity for Douglas, or so she thinks. She finds the playboy-writer not only untidy and disorganized but that she follows a long line of mistress-secretaries, some of whom still like to visit. Not prepared to contend with extra-curricular requirements, she quits. But Douglas is smitten and he pursues her, going to the extreme length of offering marriage. Once married, they retire to a cabin in the mountains, where both husband and wife go about writing novels. The balloon of bliss bursts when publishers turn down Douglas' book but readily accept the first effort by his wife. Professional rivalry is too great a burden for the marriage and the pair separates.

The wife, truly in love with her husband, withholds her book for a while, hoping to bring about a

With Gale Robbins

With Keenan Wynn and Laraine Day

reconciliation, but eventually she lets it be published. It wins an award and Douglas is impressed, and through the machinations of their friends the couple is re-united. Douglas and Day play the parts with a sparkle that compensates for the thin material, greatly aided by a platoon of funny character actors. At best *My Dear Secretary* is a farce, amusing but mild.

With Russell Hicks

With Keenan Wynn, Helen Walker, Laraine Day and Rudy Vallee

With Ann Sothern

A Letter to Three Wives

1948   A 20th Century-Fox Film. *Produced by* Sol C. Siegel. *Directed and written by* Joseph L. Mankiewicz. *Adapted by* Vera Caspary *from the novel by* John Klempner. *Photographed by* Arthur Miller. *Edited by* J. Watson Webb, Jr. *Art directors,* Lyle Wheeler and J. Russell Spencer. *Musical score by* Alfred Newman. *Running time:* 103 minutes.

CAST: Jeanne Crain *(Deborah Bishop),* Linda Darnell *(Lora May Hollingsway),* Ann Sothern *(Rita Phipps),* Kirk Douglas *(George Phipps),* Paul Douglas *(Porter Hollingsway),* Barbara Lawrence *(Babe),* Jeffrey Lynn *(Brad Bishop),* Connie Gilchrist *(Mrs. Finney),* Florence Bates *(Mrs. Manleigh),* Hobart Cavanaugh *(Mr. Manleigh),* Patti Brady *(Kathleen),* Ruth Vivian *(Miss Hawkins),* Thelma Ritter *(Sadie),* Stuart Holmes *(Old Man),* George Offerman, Jr. *(Nick),* Ralph Brooks *(Character),* James Adamson *(Butler),* Joe Bautista *(Thomasino),* John Davidson *(Waiter),* Carl Switzer *(Messenger).*

Joseph L. Mankiewicz won two Oscars for his *A Letter to Three Wives,* one for writing it and the other for directing it, and it has yet to be excelled as a gentle, witty, civilized comedy on the foibles of marriage.

It is actually an examination of three marriages in a small Hudson Valley town, as the wives, thinking their unions are in peril, look back and try to understand why and how they might have failed. The Mankiewicz story thankfully avoids tired stereotypes of the American male, who is all too often presented as a nice but dim-witted fumbler in comedies of this kind. None of Mankiewicz' husbands is hen-pecked and each is a well-adjusted, relatively normal man. It is the wives, each attractive and each complacent in her marital security, who come in for scrutiny here.

With Ann Sothern and Jeanne Crain

The casting is excellent. Jeanne Crain is paired with Jeffrey Lynn, Linda Darnell with Paul Douglas, and Ann Sothern with Kirk Douglas. The catalyst in the Mankiewicz plot is a woman called Addie Ross, an acquaintance of the three wives. She is never seen by the audience but heard throughout the picture as a narrator. The voice belongs to Celeste Holm, who somewhat sardonically sets up the character of the town and the characters in it.

At the outset, the three wives are seen about to embark on a river trip as chaperones to a party of youngsters. Before the steamer has left the dock, each has received and read a letter from Addie. The letters have a common message—that by the end of the day, Addie will leave town and take with her one of the three husbands, but not saying which one. As each of the wives ponder the problem, their home lives are revealed in a series of flashbacks. Jeanne Crain is an overly possessive wife, insecure from the start of her marriage. She is seen being brought to the town, a Navy WAVE, by her naval officer husband. Eventually she settles down, but

With Jeanne Crain, Jeffrey Lynn and Ann Sothern

With Jeanne Crain

With Ann Sothern

never quite overcomes a sense of awkwardness, which causes her to hang on to her handsome husband a little too tightly.

A wife of a different kind is Linda Darnell. A pretty, flirtatious and shrewd girl from the other side of the tracks, she sets her sights on wealthy businessman Paul Douglas. He's a rough-hewn type and no match for the sly minx who nails him. Thus Darnell finds material security in marriage but it occurs to her, on reflection, that she is smug about her success and should perhaps be more appreciative.

The most interesting couple of *A Letter to Three Wives* is the Ann Sothern–Kirk Douglas duo, a radio script writer wife and an English literature teacher husband. Sothern is an overly confident woman who makes far more money than her husband; she tries to steer him away from Shakespeare and join her in the more lucrative field of soap opera. In love though they are, she tends to push a little too hard and he tends to bristle. In one especially good scene, she stages a dinner party and invites her sponsors, a forceful married couple for whom soap opera is a way of life, to try to inveigle her husband into their ranks. Instead, he parries with cutting comments about these "amazing-human-documents-tune-in-tomorrow-night-to-see-what happens" programs. After the exasperated guests leave, Douglas wastes no time telling his wife that he is tired of watching such an intelligent woman turn into a "fearful, sniveling writer of drooling pap."

With Jeanne Crain and Ann Sothern

On the steamer cruising the river, the three wives each arrive at the conclusion that she has lost her marriage. As it turns out, none has. A deft plot ploy by Mankiewicz effects a happy ending, and one that, for the benefit of those who have not seen this enjoyable picture, should be left unrevealed. Mankiewicz' film almost defies criticism. For Kirk Douglas it was his first exposure on screen in a truly likable and believable part, and one which could not help but advance his career.

Champion

1949   A Screen Plays Production, *distributed by* United Artists. *Produced by* Stanley Kramer. *Directed by* Mark Robson. *Written by* Carl Foreman, *adapted from a story by* Ring Lardner. *Photographed by* Frank Planer. *Edited by* Harry Gerstad. *Musical score by* Dimitri Tiomkin. *Running time:* 99 minutes.

CAST: Kirk Douglas *(Midge Kelly)*, Marilyn Maxwell *(Grace Diamond)*, Arthur Kennedy *(Connie Kelly)*, Paul Stewart *(Tommy Haley)*, Ruth Roman *(Emma Bryce)*, Lola Albright *(Mrs. Harris [Palmer])*, Luis Van Rooten *(Jerome Harris)*, John Day *(Johnny Dunne)*, Harry Shannon *(Lew Bryce)*.

Kirk Douglas was next scheduled to appear in *The Great Sinner,* a costume melodrama at MGM, starring Gregory Peck and Ava Gardner. His agent had set a good price on the actor's services, and the role was thought to be a solid stepping stone in a steadily advancing career. But Douglas had not been satisfied with the speed of his progress in Hollywood and when Stanley Kramer, then at the start of his course as an independent producer, offered him top billing in a boxing picture based on Ring Lardner's short story *Champion,* Douglas accepted. The Kramer picture was economically budgeted at half a million dollars and Douglas' salary was less than the MGM offer. However, Douglas sensed that *Champion* was a gamble that might pay off, and he was right. The film is a gem of its kind, and it elevated Douglas to

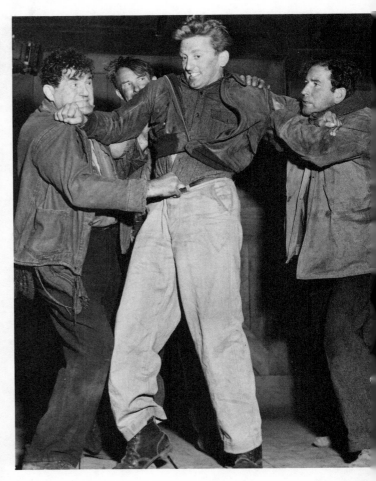

With Paul Stewart and Arthur
Kennedy

stardom and boosted the careers of Kramer and
director Mark Robson.

Champion remains an exceptional film; it is brutal, realistic and uncompromising in telling the story
of a boxer who batters his way to the top of the
business, oblivious to ethics and gratitude. While appearing as a hero to the fans, he is a viciously selfish
man to those who know him. The film, admirably
paced and developed by Robson, begins with the
night of his greatest triumph in the ring, and recounts
his story in flashbacks.

Midge Kelly (Douglas) and his crippled brother
Connie (Arthur Kennedy) make their way by railroad
boxcar to California to take over their interest in a
roadside café, acquired by Midge from a wartime
Navy chum. They are mugged and thrown off the
train by hoboes, and given a lift on the highway by a
prizefighter, Johnny Dunne (John Day), and his girl-
friend Grace (Marilyn Maxwell).

In Kansas City, encouraged by the fighter, Midge
takes a crack at earning a few badly needed dollars
by entering a boxing event, in which he is painfully
beaten. But a manager, Tommy Haley (Paul Stewart),
senses there is something about Midge and he makes
him an offer. Midge turns it down and the brothers
proceed to California, where they find their café investment to be a fraud.

Broke, they take jobs at another café, owned by
Lew Bryce (Harry Shannon) and his daughter Emma

With Paul Stewart

(Ruth Roman). Midge and the daughter are drawn to each other and the suspicious father forces them to get married. Disgusted, Midge leaves immediately after the ceremony, and accompanied by his brother, who vainly tries to make him stay, he proceeds to Los Angeles and looks up the fight manager who offered to take him on.

Within months, Midge is an acceptable boxer, coached by manager Haley in ruthless technique and

With Arthur Kennedy

taught by him that boxing is a racket in which only the ruthless survive. Midge is an eager pupil, especially once he begins to taste success.

Champion charts the course of a man determined to be a champion, no matter the cost. His social behavior is as ruthless as his fighting. When matched in the ring with Johnny Dunne, with Grace in the audience, Midge is told to throw the fight, because the "syndicate" wants it that way. When he steps into the ring he smiles at Grace, but the smile is not returned. Offended, he proceeds to win the fight by battering Dunne to a bloody hulk.

Later, hoods catch Midge and his manager and beat them. Grace is now drawn to the ambitious fighter and she brings influence to bear in having the syndicate lift their ban on Midge. This they do, provided Midge agrees to dump his manager. Midge now scales the heights, winning fight after fight, lauded by

With Marilyn Maxwell

On the set

Emma is obtaining a divorce to marry his brother. Midge appears agreeable. Months later, Midge makes a play for his ex-wife and when Connie denounces him, he is floored by the champ.

Johnny Dunne, seeking both revenge and professional reinstatement, gets a re-match with the champ whose career he initiated. Dunne discovers that Midge is not up to his old form, success has softened him. As the rounds go by, Dunne gains the upper hand and Midge takes murderous punishment. His coach begs him to throw in the towel but the desperate Midge refuses—he is determined not to be beaten. Horribly battered, his face a bloody pulp, Midge manages to summon his strength and he rocks Dunne with a mighty blow. Dunne is knocked unconscious and Midge is declared the winner. But Midge is badly hurt, and a doctor is summoned. As his feverish mind wanders, Midge imagines he is back in his first fight, hoping one day for a crack at the championship. As Connie and Emma arrive, Midge dies. Asked for a press statement, the brother decides not to disillusion the public. He says, "He was a champion, and he went out like a champion. He was a credit to the fight game to the very end."

Few actors have embraced a part as Douglas did Midge Kelly. It is a thorough performance, completely convincing in every respect and played with a ferocious forcefulness. *Champion* is a compelling film and Douglas emerges from it like a rocket. Perhaps there was an affinity between the part and the actor, in terms of ambition. With this performance, Kirk Douglas, quite literally, made himself a filmdom champ.

the press as a scrapper who never throws a contest. Less and less moral, Midge now makes a play for the beautiful wife (Lola Albright) of his new boss, as he sheds Grace. The boss, recognizing the caliber of the man, proves to his wife that Midge can be induced by money to end the affair, and he does.

Learning that their mother is dying, Midge joins Connie at her deathbed. He also learns that his wife

With Hoagy Carmichael

Young Man with a Horn

1950   A Warner Bros. Picture. *Produced by* Jerry Wald. *Directed by* Michael Curtiz. *Written by* Carl Foreman *and* Edmund H. North, *based on the novel by* Dorothy Baker. *Photographed by* Ted McCord. *Edited by* Alan Crosland, Jr. *Art director,* Edward Carrere. *Music director,* Ray Heindorf. *Running time:* 111 minutes.

CAST: Kirk Douglas *(Rick Martin),* Lauren Bacall *(Amy North),* Doris Day *(Jo Jordan),* Hoagy Carmichael *(Smoke Willoughby),* Juano Hernandez *(Art Hazzard),* Jerome Cowan *(Phil Morrison),* Mary Beth Hughes *(Margo Mar-* *tin),* Nestor Paiva *(Galba),* Orley Lindgren *(Rick* [*as a boy*]*),* Walter Reed *(Jack Chandler),* Alex Gerry *(Dr. Weaver).*

Bix Beiderbecke is a legend in American music. He was part of the groundswell of jazz that came to fruition in the Roaring Twenties, and among the many men who were dedicated to this distinctly American form of music he was considered a classicist—disciplined, subdued in his playing of the cornet and pure-of-tone in his style, all of which was in contrast to his private life. From Chicago, Beiderbecke came to prominence in 1923 when he formed The Wolverines, one of the most vital of jazz ensembles. He and

With Jerome Cowan

his group helped to make jazz history and his career would doubtless have been a long one but for his personal life. Beiderbecke drank excessively and he died in 1931 at the age of twenty-eight.

Years later novelist Dorothy Baker used his life story as the basis for her *Young Man With a Horn.* Warner Bros. bought the film rights to the novel in 1945 but delayed filming it until they could find an actor suitable for the leading role. The success of Kirk Douglas in *Champion* solved the matter; here was the perfect challenger to play the sensitive but

With Hoagy Carmichael

compulsive musician. However, the film is not, and wasn't meant to be, a portrait of Beiderbecke, but only of that kind of man. And whereas the musician in Miss Baker's novel dies. Warner Bros. opted for a happy ending, albeit an obviously contrived one.

Warners had the happy inspiration of hiring Hoagy Carmichael to play the on-screen role of narrator and best friend of the title musician. The song writer had in fact been a close friend and colleague of Bix Beiderbecke, and knew the subject and the musical milieu better than most people. Also, Carmichael's laconic style as an actor, his drawling voice, not to mention his ability with a piano and a song, gives *Young Man With a Horn* a marvelous aura of authenticity.

The film begins with Carmichael, as a veteran jazz musician named Smoke Willoughby, sitting at the piano and reminiscing about Rick Martin (Douglas), a boy who wanted to grow up to be the best trumpet player in the world. At the age of ten, Rick was a sensitive boy left much to himself after the death of his mother. Magnetically drawn to music, the boy wanders into Skid Row taverns to listen to pianos being played. In a smoky dive called the Cotton Club he discovers a five-piece jazz band lead by Art Hazzard (Juano Hernandez).

Young Rick becomes infatuated with the Negro jazz musician, and he takes a job as a pinboy in a bowling alley in order to save up fourteen dollars to buy an old trumpet. Hazzard becomes the most important person in the boy's life, with the old musician teaching him everything he knows about music.

Years later, when Hazzard goes on the road,

Rick, now twenty, gets his first job, playing trumpet in a dance band and it is here he meets two people who will be greatly important in his life, pianist Smoke Willoughby and singer Jo Jordan (Doris Day). Rick gets off to a bad start with the band leader by playing the music as he *feels* it, rather than the way it is written. Both Rick and Smoke are fired a few nights later for their insistence on introducing jazz style into their playing. They spend the next few months playing their kind of music at a succession of dives and honky-tonks, until Smoke gets tired of the sleazy places in which they play, especially after a run-in with gunmen, and decides to go back to his hometown in Indiana. Rick then heads for New York, and re-discovers Jo, now singing with another band. She then takes him to a small jazz café where Art Hazzard is playing, and it comes as a shock to Rick to find his old friend ailing and no longer able to play well. Rick steps up and takes over, playing brilliantly. This leads to a job with a major dance band, of which he quickly becomes the stellar attraction.

One night, Jo introduces Rick to Amy North (Lauren Bacall), a wealthy, bored girl of strange appeal. Rick becomes fascinated with Amy and they are soon lovers, with the musician neglecting his work and his old friends. Once married, their love subsides and Rick finds himself caught in a luxurious trap—his wife has no real interest in music and she prefers her own interests and level of society. Rick takes to

drinking. He is brought to his senses by the death of Art Hazzard, killed when struck by a car. He goes to the funeral in a little Negro church and during the ceremony he picks up Art's trumpet and plays it, expressing his sorrow and his grief. Returning to his wife, Rick finds her irate because he has missed one

With Doris Day and Lauren Bacall

of her parties; in a rage she smashes his collection of jazz records and tells him she is sick of the sound of his music.

The break-up of his marriage sends Rick further down the alcoholic road. He loses his job with the band and begins to play in a variety of dives until his health breaks and he collapses. Smoke and Jo find him and revive him in time to keep a recording date. Rick plays well at the session until he has to hit a high note—a note he has always wanted to hit. He fails, and after repeated, furious attempts he smashes his trumpet against a wall. After this, Rick begins to fall apart, he again takes to the dive circuit, sinking lower in prestige and health as he goes. One day, in a sober moment, he buys a trumpet in a pawn shop. A little later he stumbles in the street and a taxi runs over the trumpet; the driver picks up Rick and takes him to a cheap hospital for alcoholics. Smoke and Jo manage to locate him and transfer him to a better hospital. As he hears the sound of the ambulance siren, Rick admits that the wail hits the note he has never been able to hit. The film ends philosophically with Smoke Willoughby telling us: "Rick learned that you can't say everything through the end of a trumpet, and that a man doesn't destroy himself because he can't hit some high note he dreamed up."

Young Man With a Horn is a film with a definite style. It is, of course, of particular appeal to lovers of jazz but it also holds firm as a story under the hand of master director Michael Curtiz. It contains a great deal of music, including a half-dozen standard songs

sung by Doris Day. Understandably, it is the trumpet work that really shines and gives the picture its impact. Harry James was hired as musical advisor and it is James who is heard as Kirk Douglas fakes the playing. Douglas approached the trumpet study with his usual brand of determination. Coached by Warner's studio orchestra trumpeter Larry Sullivan, Douglas worked with the instrument over a three-month period, learning to finger the valves and purse his lips like an expert, and becoming a competent player. Such was his zeal that Curtiz finally had to ask Douglas to stop playing the instrument in his dressing room, because it was disturbing the company.

With Hoagy Carmichael

The Glass Menagerie

1950   A Warner Bros Picture. *Produced by* Jerry Wald *and* Charles K. Feldman. *Directed by* Irving Rapper. *Written by* Tennessee Williams *and* Peter Berneis, *based on the play by* Williams. *Photographed by* Robert Burks. *Edited by* David Weisbart. *Art director,* Robert Haas. *Musical score by* Max Steiner. *Running time:* 106 minutes.

CAST: Jane Wyman *(Laura),* Kirk Douglas *(Jim),* Gertrude Lawrence *(Amanda),* Arthur Kennedy *(Tom),* Ralph Sanford *(Mendoza),* Ann Tyrrell *(Clerk),* John Compton *(Young Man),* Gertrude Graner *(Woman Instructor),* Sara Edwards *(Mrs. Miller),* Louise Lorri-

mer *(Miss Porter),* Cris Alcaide *(Eddie),* Perdita Chandler *(A Girl).*

Tennessee Williams won the New York Drama Critics Circle award for his *The Glass Menagerie,* and it has remained one of the most popular of American plays, especially with amateur theatrical groups who find it a perfect vehicle for studying and performing. A simple story about four people—a proud mother, a crippled, introspective daughter, a discontented son, and a "gentleman caller"—each of the characters is deeply and richly etched. Aided by Peter Berneis, Williams adapted the play into a film scenario and watched with approval as the story was carefully and tastefully transferred to the screen. The result was a

With Arthur Kennedy

delightful film that manages not to look like a filmed stage play. Opened up to include scenes in various locations, it loses none of the intimacy of the original stage one-setting, thanks largely to the sensitivity of director Irving Rapper.

As the film opens we see the shabby apartment of middle-aged Amanda Wingfield (Gertrude Lawrence) in a tenement district of St. Louis. Her husband, "a telephone man who fell in love with long distance," has long fled. Amanda was once, as she tells it, a southern belle besieged by "gentleman callers." She keeps the home together from the small wages earned by Tom (Arthur Kennedy), a warehouseman who hates his job and writes poetry as an escape. Amanda is a woman of vitality but she is nagging and pretentious as she hounds her children to better them-

With Jane Wyman and Arthur Kennedy

With Gertrude Lawrence, Jane Wyman and Arthur Kennedy

With Jane Wyman

selves. Tom bristles at the nagging and Laura (Jane Wyman) withdraws from reality and finds comfort in her "glass menagerie," (a collection of glass figurines) and in listening to music on the phonograph. Amanda attempts to enroll Laura in a typing school, but the frightened, crippled girl leaves after one fumbling lesson. Her mother then resolves that if the girl cannot make her own way in the world, she must find a husband, and she nags Tom into bringing home a friend from the warehouse.

Tom invites Jim O'Connor (Kirk Douglas), a nice, ordinary young man—and unsuspecting. Amanda makes preparations for the visit and spends money she can ill afford to refurbish her apartment, setting the scene for what she hopes will be a romance.

When Jim arrives, Laura recognizes him as a boy she secretly loved in high school. While the two sit alone in the living room, Jim tries to draw out the shy, gentle girl. He flatters her and after proving to her she can dance if she tries, he takes her to a near-by dance hall. There he insists that Laura dance with him, and tenderly he gives her her first kiss. Jim soon senses he has gone too far. In trying to help her he has caused her to fall in love with him. Afraid to hurt her further, Jim confesses he is already engaged. Laura is crushed, but on reflection she realizes the experience has helped cure her of her shyness and her introspection, and helped her realize that having a lame leg is not the handicap she had imagined it to be.

With Jane Wyman

After the "gentleman caller" leaves, Amanda rebukes her long-suffering son for bringing home an engaged man instead of an eligible one. She berates him for "making up dreams" and "manufacturing illusions," precisely the things of which she is guilty herself. This is the last straw for Tom, who now leaves home and goes to sea, as he has long wanted to do. He asks Laura to forgive him and he promises to send home money every month. In a montage sequence, we see Tom in various ports, "attempting to find in motion what was lost in space." At the end we see Laura, now a more happy and confident girl, sitting on the fire escape with Amanda and awaiting the arrival of a new "gentleman caller"—the "long delayed but always expected something that we live for."

The Glass Menagerie is a warm and compelling picture but not, as the producers would discover, a greatly commercial one. There is, regrettably, a wide difference in the acceptance level of stage and movie audiences—or at least there was in 1950. It is, however, hard to find fault with this film. As the delicate Laura, Jane Wyman is touchingly vulnerable and wistful, and Gertrude Lawrence conveys the drive and the infuriating delusiveness of the overly protective, loving mother, although the British actress has the problem of playing with an assumed Southern accent. Arthur Kennedy, an actor who has managed to divide his career between the stage and the screen, brings every last ounce of anguish to the role of the frustrated brother. Kirk Douglas, in the smallest role in the quartet, is perfect as the decent-minded warehouse worker who walks into the situation quite innocently but who leaves having after unwittingly changed the lives of the others. The film is also greatly aided by the expertise of its technical crew; by the muted photography of Robert Burks, the convincing sets of Robert Haas, and the gentle, brooding musical score of Max Steiner.

With Jane Wyman

Ace in the Hole

1951 A Paramount Production, *distributed by* Paramount. *Produced and directed by* Billy Wilder. *Written by* Billy Wilder, Lesser Samuels *and* Walter Newman. *Photographed by* Charles Lang, Jr. *Edited by* Doane Harrison *and* Arthur Schmidt. *Art directors,* Hal Pereira *and* Earl Hedrick. *Musical score by* Hugo Friedhofer. *Running time:* 111 minutes.

CAST: Kirk Douglas *(Charles Tatum),* Jan Sterling *(Lorraine),* Bob Arthur *(Herbie Cook),* Porter Hall *(Jacob Q. Boot),* Frank Cady *(Mr.* *Federber),* Richard Benedict *(Leo Minosa),* Ray Teal *(Sheriff),* Lewis Martin *(McCardle),* John Berkes *(Papa Minosa),* Frances Dominguez *(Mama Minosa),* Gene Evans *(Deputy Sheriff),* Frank Jaquet *(Smollett),* Harry Harvey *(Dr. Hilton),* Bob Bumpas *(Radio Announcer),* Geraldine Hall *(Mrs. Federber),* Richard Ganes *(Nagel).*

To understand *Ace in the Hole* requires some knowledge of the man who made it, Billy Wilder. Wilder produced and directed the picture and also co-scripted it with Lesser Samuels and Walter Newman,

With Porter Hall

and it is very much a film with a personal stamp. Brilliant though *Ace in the Hole* is, the humor is black. Wilder is noted among his colleagues as a man of mordant wit and quite often cruel in his barbed, devastating observations of humankind.

Wilder scowls at the world. Born in Vienna in 1906, he cut his professional teeth in Berlin as a film writer and left there in 1933 because of the Nazis. He went first to Paris and then to California.

Writer Wilder turned director in 1942 but he has also been involved with the scripts of all the films he has directed. His biggest successes have been *Double Indemnity, The Lost Weekend, A Foreign Affair, Sunset Boulevard, The Apartment,* and *Some Like it Hot.* In every case, these films have been marked by incisive, harsh revelations of human weaknesses, although very often couched in the form of comedy. It is a jaundiced view, saved from being repugnant

With Bob Arthur

With Jan Sterling

by Wilder's ability to entertain and fascinate. But in the case of *Ace in the Hole,* his contempt overcame his judgment and the result is a bitter film.

The story is set in New Mexico, partly in Albuquerque and partly in the nearby mountains. Charles Tatum (Kirk Douglas) is a reporter on the local paper, and a man down on his professional luck, due to his drinking and his lack of ethics. His idea is to somehow turn out a story that will put him back in

the journalistic big-time. Such an opportunity comes his way: en route to cover a rattlesnake hunt with a cub reporter, Herbie Cook (Robert Arthur), they come across a man buried alive in a cave-in. The man is trapped while searching for Indian relics in a mountain area considered by the Indians as being sacred. Tatum spots his chance. Rather than facilitate the rescue of Leo Minosa (Richard Benedict), the reporter decides to play out the drama of the situation. He persuades the local sheriff (Ray Teal) that the ensuing publicity will help his forthcoming election campaign, and the sheriff agrees to keep other reporters away from the site. Thus Tatum has an exclusive.

Tatum burrows his way to the doomed man, thereby giving his reportage an added fillip of heroism. When a rescue team of miners point out that it is possible to shore up the tunnel and get Minosa out, Tatum talks the foreman into a more devious route, drilling down from above. News of the operation quickly fills the newspapers and the airwaves, and within a day thousands of curiosity seekers descend on the area. A car park is set up, and concessionaires move in with food stands and entertainment. Tatum locates Minosa's wife, Lorraine (Jan Sterling) and finds her to be a sluttish waitress, unconcerned about her husband and ready to leave town. Tatum inveigles her into staying, pointing out the money she might make selling refreshments to the crowds. He also asks her to go to church, so he can get a photo of her praying, but she replies, "I don't pray. Kneeling bags my nylons."

The scene of the rescue site soon turns into a carnival—a monstrous charade in the shadow of the dying man, complete with a Ferris wheel, TV coverage, a press tent, food and drink stalls, and a song written for the occasion, "We're Coming Leo," sung by a chorus of tourists so that Minosa can hear it, as does the huge radio and TV audience. Tatum spins out his wicked piece of sensationalism for a week, but it is all in vain. Minosa dies, and in an ending that is far from plausible, Tatum is stricken with feelings of guilt. Wilder then, possibly realizing the enormity of his ghastly story, has the wife kill Tatum by sticking a knife in him in a restaurant. But by then, it is too late to alter the course of *Ace in the Hole,* the vicious die is cast. What emerges is a technically stunning picture about a digusting situation.

Perhaps neither Wilder nor Paramount had given much thought to the fact that this, and all films, needed the support of the press to get its reviews. Journalists were offended by the depiction of Tatum as such an ugly brute, and many made the point that it was unlikely that a reporter could get away with such a device. Unfortunately, the public tended to

With Richard Benedict

feel the same way about *Ace in the Hole*—it was just too searing to be entertaining. The Paramount publicists made a point of courting the press, and the title was later changed to *The Big Carnival,* but nothing made the film palatable. In view of the quality of the film, this is regrettable, especially for Kirk Douglas who here turned in a glowing, albeit evil, performance as the sleazy, enterprising but heartless Tatum. However, the film is not completely lost, it is a favorite among film study groups and it turns up in festivals of movie retrospection particularly those dealing with the work of Wilder and Douglas.

It is difficult to think of a Hollywood film more uncompromising in its attitude toward its subject, and therefore so limited in its commercial appeal. *Ace in the Hole* is a Wilder baby from conception to deliverance, and one that caused him some embarrassment. It was two years before he made his next picture, *Stalag 17,* and although it and subsequent Wilder films deal with the various frailties of the human animal, he has been careful to disguise his rage with copious waves of laughter. Wilder found with *Ace in the Hole* that the audience doesn't like to feel part of the indictment.

With Billy Wilder

With Virginia Mayo

Along the Great Divide

1951   A Warner Bros. Picture. *Produced by* Anthony Veiller. *Directed by* Raoul Walsh. *Written by* Walter Doniger *and* Lewis Meltzer, *based on a story by* Doniger. *Photographed by* Sid Hickox. *Edited by* Thomas Reilly. *Art director,* Edward Carrere. *Musical score by* David Buttolph. *Running time:* 88 minutes.

CAST: Kirk Douglas *(Len Merrick),* Virginia Mayo *(Ann Keith),* John Agar *(Billy Shear),* Walter Brennan *(Pop Keith),* Ray Teal *(Lou Gray),* Hugh Sanders *(Frank Newcombe),* Morris Ankrum *(Ed Roden),* James Anderson *(Dan Roden),* Charles Meredith *(The Judge).*

Kirk Douglas' first western was a slickly produced but conventional specimen and he was clearly not at ease in this new, but inevitable, avenue of his movie career. As he had learned to box and to play the trumpet for previous assignments, so Douglas learned how to ride a horse and how to handle six-guns for *Along the Great Divide,* and in so doing discovered an enjoyment in this kind of film making. The eastern dude quickly became a western pro. He had the considerable help of Raoul Walsh, a veteran director of action-adventure films, but the story line of this picture is pulp magazine material and hard to swallow.

Douglas appears here as a newly elected U.S. Marshal named Len Merrick. In the company of two deputies, Billy Shear (John Agar) and Lou Gray (Ray Teal), he breaks up a group about to lynch old Pop Keith (Walter Brennan), whom rancher Ed Roden (Morris Ankrum) believes to be the murderer of his son Ed Jr. Aiding him is his other son, Dan (James Anderson). Merrick and his deputies take Pop into

With Walter Brennan

safekeeping, and then start to transport him across miles of open country to the town of Santa Loma where he will stand trial. The film is largely an accounting of what happens along the way. First, Merrick visits the scene of the crime and there, while poking around, finds a watch.

Marshal Merrick returns to the shack in which his prisoner and his deputies have put up for the night and finds it being fired upon by a gunman. Overpowering the gunman, he finds him to be a beautiful young girl, Ann (Virginia Mayo), the daughter of his grizzled old prisoner. Warned by a local rancher that Roden intends to stop the trip to justice, Merrick and his group set off immediately. During the long journey it is revealed that the marshal is a complicated man, beset with fears that he might have caused the death of his father, also a marshal. Once Pop picks up this tidbit of information he uses it to taunt Merrick. The group is attacked by Roden as they plod across the burning sands, having taken the desert route as a

With Walter Brennan and Virginia Mayo

With Virginia Mayo, James Anderson, Walter Brennan and Ray Teal

shortcut, and deputy Billy is fatally wounded. But Merrick manages to capture Dan Roden and takes him along as a safeguard that the elder Roden will not attack again.

The trip across the desert becomes increasingly arduous as their water supply diminishes and the heat bears down on them. The weary group begin to falter. Dan Roden inveigles Deputy Lou into switching his allegiance but when the pair finally get the drop on the marshal, Pop comes to the aid of the lawman and

saves his life, shooting the deputy in the process. On the survivors trudge, with Ann and Merrick now enamored of each other.

Finally, Merrick and his half-dead band stagger into Santa Loma. Pop is tried and quickly found guilty, to the chagrin of Merrick who now believes him innocent. Irate, he rips his marshal's badge from his chest, causing the watch, found at the scene of the crime, to fall to the floor and break open. Inside Merrick spots an inscription, which proves the watch

With Walter Brennan

With Virginia Mayo, Walter Brennan, Ray Teal and John Agar

to be the property of Dan Roden. His father, on hand to witness the hanging, verifies this. It is then apparent that Dan is guilty of fratricide, and in the subsequent chase and cornering, Merrick shoots and kills Dan. At fade out, Merrick and Ann ride off together, obviously destined for a distant altar, with old Pop trailing along.

Along the Great Divide is best described as competent in all departments, and excellent in only one

respect—the photography of the veteran Sid Hickox. The fine location shooting was done partly in the High Sierra country in the vicinity of Lone Pine, California, and partly in the Mojave desert area some thirty miles south of Lone Pine. The stark beauty of the desert lands, pictured by Hickox, give the film its only distinction. But Kirk Douglas would not have to wait long before finding western vehicles of real pith and punch.

With James Anderson, Ray Teal and Walter Brennan

Detective Story

1951   A William Wyler Production, *distributed by* Paramount. *Directed by* William Wyler. *Written by* Philip Yordan *and* Robert Wyler, *based on the play by* Sidney Kingsley. *Photographed by* Lee Garmes. *Edited by* Robert Swink. *Art directors,* Hal Pereira *and* Earl Hedrick. *Running time:* 105 minutes.

CAST: Kirk Douglas *(Detective James McLeod)*, Eleanor Parker *(Mary McLeod)*, William Bendix *(Detective Lou Brody)*, Lee Grant *(A Shoplifter)*, Bert Freed *(Detective Dakis)*, Frank Faylen *(Detective Gallagher)*, Grandon Rhodes *(Detective O'Brien)*, Luis Van Rooten *(Police Reporter)*, Craig Hill *(Arthur Kindred)*, Cathy O'Donnell *(Susan Carmichael,* Horace McMahon *(Lt. Monaghan)*, Warner Anderson *(Endicott Sims)*, George Macready *(Karl Schneider)*, Joseph Wiseman *(Charles Gennini)*, Michael Strong *(Lewis Abbott)*, Russell Evans *(Patrolman Barnes)*, Howard Joslyn *(Patrolman Keogh)*, Gladys George *(Miss Hatch)*, Burt Mustin *(Janitor)*, James Maloney *(Mrs. Pritchett)*, Gerald Mohr *(Tami Giacopetti)*.

Producer-director William Wyler claims that his main interest in making a film from Sidney Kingley's play *Detective Story* was the challenge of transferring it to the screen without changing it drastically, without moving outside the one-set structure of the original. Wyler succeeded brilliantly; except for one sequence in a police wagon, the film stays within the confines of its set, a New York police station, and yet so well and quickly paced is the story and its fascinating parade of characters that Wyler's picture never gives

With William Bendix

With Cathy O'Donnell and Craig Hill

the impression of being a filmed play. This is also due to the expert camera work of the veteran Lee Garmes, whose fluid, restless lensing keeps the images flowing, a not inconsiderable accomplishment for such a long session on one set. The wise Wyler also brought in many players from the original New York cast of *Detective Story,* actors whose familiarity with the material doubtless contributed to the facility of filming it. Two of the New York actors here made their film debuts—Joseph Wiseman, as a demented, homicidal burglar, and Lee Grant, as a jaunty, Brooklynese shoplifter. Both were lauded for their work in

this film and both received further offers to work in Hollywood; Wiseman accepted those offers that interested him and enabled him to continue his stage career, but Miss Grant elected not to appear in another film until fourteen years later.

Detective Story is not so much a tale of detection but a focusing on the life and character of just one detective, James McLeod (Kirk Douglas). McLeod is no ordinary detective, he is a fanatic, dedicated to the law and excessively brutal in dealing with criminals. He is particularly upset about abortionists, and it gradually becomes apparent that this is a psycho-

With George Macready

With Eleanor Parker

logical block in his mind. Some tragic happening in his past has caused him to look upon abortionists in a pathological light, and the abortionist in this film, played by George Macready with his patent brand of quiet, sinister refinement, has a hard time in the hands of McLeod. The abortion angle of the original play was broadened for the film, partly because of censorship, and partly because the close-up, immedi-

acy of the camera requires rage to be clearly more explained than on the stage. Hence, the film abortionist is also the manipulator of an adoption ring and a farm for unwed mothers. Whenever he appears at the precinct the abortionist is accompanied by his lawyer, although he might also have hired a body-guard, since the fist-swinging McLeod is not above belting his suspects. As the story progresses, the reasons for McLeod's vicious temper and his hatred for crime are revealed as stemming from his love-hate attitude toward his father, a man of crooked tendencies. His mania makes life hard for his gentle wife Mary (Eleanor Parker) to whom he is nevertheless greatly attached.

With Joseph Wiseman

With Joseph Wiseman

Detective McLeod is understandably shattered when he discovers that his wife was once herself the subject of an abortion, and that the man who performed the illegal operation was the abortionist now at his mercy, Karl Schneider (Macready). McLeod cannot bring himself to forgive his wife, his anger and his confusion are so great that he deliberately exposes himself to death. He steps into the line of fire of a desperate hoodlum who pulls a gun in an attempt to escape from the station. As McLeod lies dying, he recites the Act of Contrition.

Detective Story is light on plot line but rich in its myriad cast of characters. It is, in fact, a series of character studies, one major and many minor. Kirk Douglas carries the burden of McLeod and makes the tormented policeman painfully believable—it is almost a nonstop, swirling performance. Around him Wyler arrays an expert team of players: William Bendix as a tough but warm-hearted veteran cop; Horace Mc-Mahon as the precinct lieutenant who tolerates the frenzy of McLeod because he realizes he is doing his job honestly and well, if overzealously; Eleanor Parker as the wife, driven to near-distraction by her husband; and several weirdly amusing criminal types, of whom those played by Wiseman and Miss Grant are shining examples, all of them moving through the grimey, harshly realistic atmosphere of a police station on any given work day. The realism of the film is also due in part to the sets built by art directors Hal Pereira and Earl Hedrick, whose creation on a Paramount sound stage might easily have passed for

the real thing. Wyler also decided not to use a music score, except for that accompanying the credit titles. Scoring invariably helps a picture but in this instance it would probably have reduced the air of reality.

To gear himself for the strenuous role of Detective McLeod, Kirk Douglas did two things. First he went to New York and spent several days and nights at the 16th Precinct, soaking up atmosphere. Then he asked Wyler's associate producer Willie Schorr to arrange for the Kingsley play to be staged at the Sombrero Playhouse in Phoenix, Arizona, with himself heading the company. The results are plainly obvious in this excellent film.

With William Bendix and Joseph Wiseman

The Big Trees

1952   A Warner Bros. Picture. *Produced by* Louis F. Edelman. *Directed by* Felix Feist. *Written by* John Twist *and* James R. Webb, *based on a story by* Kenneth Earl. *Photographed in Technicolor by* Bert Glennon. *Edited by* Clarence Kolster. *Art director,* Edward Carrere. *Musical score by* Heinz Roemheld. *Running time:* 89 minutes.

CAST: Kirk Douglas *(Jim Fallon)*, Eve Miller *(Alicia Chadwick)*, Patrice Wymore *(Daisy Fisher)*, Edgar Buchanan *(Yukon Burns)*, John Archer *(Frenchy LeCroix)*, Alan Hale, Jr. *(Tiny)*, Roy Roberts *(Judge Crenshaw)*, Charles Meredith *(Elder Bixby)*, Harry Cording *(Cleve Gregg)*, Ellen Corby *(Mrs. Blackburn)*.

Kirk Douglas was not pleased with his association with Warner Bros. It had started off well with *Young Man With a Horn,* but *The Glass Menagerie* had not been the box-office winner he had hoped and *Along the Great Divide* was clearly a limp vehicle. Douglas' contract with Warners called for nine pictures but he offered to make one for them at no salary if they would let him out of the contract. Warners took him at his word and the result was *The Big Trees.*

With or without salary, Warners should have in-

With Eve Miller

vested the picture with a better script. While it starts off promisingly, *The Big Trees* soon sinks in a morass of strained plot devices, stock characterizations and banal dialogue. In playing a slick, unscrupulous, man-of-purpose confidence trickster Douglas was given a role no actor could make likable, even though the intent of the film is to have him emerge as a likable rogue who turns heroic and ends up marrying a woman of dedicated religious bent. The character is

not without interest—a 1900 promoter who arrives in northern California, determined to make a fortune out of the immense redwood forests. The pity is that Warners wasted the premise, and Bert Glennon's fine color photography of the handsome scenery, on a mish-mash of a production.

The Big Trees hinges its plot on an interesting historical fact—that the U.S. Government in 1900 rescinded the Stone and Timber Act of 1865 and that people who had filed their land claims under that act were no longer legally entitled to their property. Inevitably, a smooth operator (Douglas) arrives in the area near Eureka, California, to push a religious sect off valuable lumber land. He reckons without the morals of his grizzled old ex-Alaska sourdough employee (Edgar Buchanan) who switches to the side of the law and becomes town marshal, and the resourcefulness of a pretty widow (Eve Miller) who burns down the Land Office containing Douglas' land applications. Neither does he reckon with other unscrupulous timber-hungry promoters, one of whom is his own gang-boss (John Archer). Things get even tougher for him when his long time, flippantly treated, dance hall singer girl friend (Patrice Wymore) sells out to the opposition by letting them have the Doug-

With Patrice Wymore, Eve Miller and Edgar Buchanan

With Roy Roberts, Edgar Buchanan, Harry Cording and John Archer las holdings signed in her name, including a dam. If Douglas were the villain of *The Big Trees,* all the miserable things that happen to him would be justified, but he is The Hero and he has only the last reel to atone for his wrongs and route the film's real villains. His adventures include rousing the religious sect to martial action and leading them against the wrongdoers, and rescuing the heroine from a runaway train headed for a sabotaged bridge. It is all too pat to be either plausible or entertaining, and the viewer is left wishing the producers had devoted more footage to the magnificent giant Sequoias among which the story takes place.

Warners sent their cast and crew to northern California for three weeks of location shooting, but they also indulged in production short cuts by incorporating footage from their 1938 picture *Valley of the Giants.* One sequence of *The Big Trees* lingers in the mind, in which an elder of the religious sect explains his veneration of the huge, ancient redwoods and shows Douglas the smooth surface of a vast tree stump, pointing out the positions of grain-rings at various times in history over the past two thousand years. Would that the rest of the film matched the quality of this moment.

With Eve Miller

The Big Sky

1952 A Winchester Pictures Production, *distributed by* RKO Radio. *Produced and directed by* Howard Hawks. *Written by* Dudley Nichols, *based on the novel by* A. B. Guthrie, Jr. *Photographed by* Russell Harlan. *Edited by* Christian Nyby. *Art directors,* Albert D'Agostino *and* Perry Ferguson. *Musical score by* Dimitri Tiomkin. *Running time:* 140 minutes.

CAST: Kirk Douglas *(Deakins)*, Dewey Martin *(Boone)*, Elizabeth Threatt *(Teal Eye)*, Arthur Hunnicutt *(Zeb)*, Buddy Baer *(Romaine)*, Steven Geray *(Jourdonnais)*, Hank Worden *(Poordevil)*, Jim Davis *(Streak)*, Henri Letondal *(Ladadie)*, Robert Hunter *(Chouquette)*, Both Colman *(Pascal)*, Paul Frees *(MacMasters)*, Frank de Kova *(Moleface)*, Guy Wilkerson *(Longface)*.

The Big Sky is far from being the most successful of Howard Hawks' westerns but it is among the most interesting films of this type. Hawks' John Wayne epics, all solid box-office winners, stylishly follow the fictional line whereas *The Big Sky* tells, and handsomely shows, something of the life of frontiersmen in the early nineteenth century as they explore the vast uncharted lands of the northwest. The film is only categorically a western, it has nothing to do with cowboys and cattle ranches, in fact, these are frontiersmen who make their way on foot through the wilderness, and occasionally by boat. Howard Hawks, who produces as well as directs his films—this one was made by his own company (Winchester)—regards himself as a story teller, and he took his time about telling this one, which ran two hours and twenty minutes in its initial release. The source material is impressive—A. B. Guthrie, Jr.'s book of the same name—and Hawks hired one of Hollywood's finest writers, Dudley Nichols, to do the screenplay. If a

With Arthur Hunnicutt and Dewey
Martin

huge, outdoors picture can be described as sensitive,
then this is a case in point.

The story starts with a pair of lusty, young Ken-
tuckians, Deakins (Kirk Douglas) and Boone (Dewey
Martin) deciding to go west and look up Boone's
uncle Zeb (Arthur Hunnicutt) who lives somewhere
west of the Mississippi. The lusty lads, who seem to
enjoy drinking and brawling about as much as anything in life, reach St. Louis, then the jumping-off
spot for western travel, but get themselves involved
in a saloon ruckus which results in them being slung
into jail. By the greatest of co-incidences they find
themselves in the same cell with Uncle Zeb. The trio
are bailed out by a river-boat captain, Jourdonnais
(Steven Geray), who needs men for a trading expedition into the Blackfoot Indian country, more than a
thousand miles distant. Eager for adventure, the three
men sign on. Uncle Zeb is especially valuable since
he is an experienced guide and trader. Jourdonnais
and his band set off in their keelboat, taking with
them a beautiful young Indian princess, Teal Eye
(Elizabeth Threatt), whom Jourdonnais regards as his
safety ticket through the Blackfoot domain. The men
are instructed to keep their minds and hands off the
Princess, but the virile Boone falls in love with the
girl, and the look in her eye reveals that the feeling
is mutual.

The film graphically accounts for the hard voyage
into the wild, lonely spaciousness of the northwest

With Dewey Martin

lands. Always cautious about Indians, Jourdonnais finds his real enemy to be a large fur trading company with no interest in competition. This company has a man called Streak (Jim Davis) whose job it is to eliminate would-be competitors. Streak and his men join with a band of Crow Indians in a savage attack on the Jourdonnais party, inflicting great injury in the gruelling fight. Deakins is wounded but he and Boone and Teal Eye manage to escape into the forest. Jourdonnais, Jeb, and the survivors consider the game lost and think in terms of selling out to the opposition. A while later, Deakin and Boone re-appear and kill Streak. Eventually, the Jourdonnais expedition reaches its goal and finds a friendly welcome among the Blackfoot Indians. Trading proceeds well and profitably, and Boone and Teal Eye presumably settle down to a life together. The footloose Deakins sets his mind for further adventures.

Kirk Douglas was the only star used by Hawks in making *The Big Sky*. Second and third billing went to Dewey Martin and Elizabeth Threatt, both of them film newcomers. Martin went on to other films but Miss Threatt's career never materialized. Hawks peopled the remainder of his cast with veteran character actors, of whom by far the most memorable is Arthur

With Elizabeth Threatt

With Elizabeth Threatt and Dewey Martin

With Elizabeth Threatt and Dewey Martin

Hunnicutt as the grizzled old Uncle Zeb, although the actor was at the time a mere forty-one years of age. The bearded, drawling, Arkansas-born Hunnicutt invariably plays crusty old-timers in westerns, and does it with distinction.

One of the major attractions of *The Big Sky* is its scenery, studiously filmed in black-and-white by Russell Harlan. Most of it was shot in Grand Teton National Park; the landscapes are sprawling and awesomely lonely, although Hawks gives them a sense of lurking danger with his tales of savage Indians silently watching the expedition and likely to attack at any time. Harlan's photography is full of mood and atmosphere, as is the musical scoring of Dimitri Tiomkin. The Russian composer had just previously scored *High Noon,* for which he won two Oscars (score and song), and he had also scored Hawks' majestic western *Red River*. Later, Tiomkin would write music for a number of epic westerns and occasionally be criticized for symphonic bombast. But his music for *The Big Sky* is gentle for the most part, and exciting when it needs to be. He used several early American tunes to give an authentic flavor to the picture, including a song about whisky for Douglas and barroom balladeers to wheeze. As the happy-go-lucky Deakins, singing, brawling, and hungry for adventure in the wilds, Kirk Douglas was clearly enjoying himself. *The Big Sky,* perhaps too long and leisurely in its style, may not be to the tastes of all western fans but it is an admirable piece of visual Americana.

With Elizabeth Threatt, Arthur Hunnicutt and Dewey Martin

The Bad and the Beautiful

1952 An MGM Picture. *Produced by* John Houseman. *Directed by* Vincente Minnelli. *Written by* Charles Schnee, *based on a story by* George Bradshaw. *Photographed by* Robert Surtees. *Edited by* Conrad A. Nervig. *Art directors,* Cedric Gibbons *and* Edward Carfagno. *Musical score by* David Raksin. *Running time:* 116 minutes.

CAST: Lana Turner *(Georgia Lorrison),* Kirk Douglas *(Jonathan Shields),* Walter Pidgeon *(Harry Pebbel),* Dick Powell *(James Lee Bartlow),* Barry Sullivan *(Fred Amiel),* Gloria Grahame *(Rosemary Bartlow),* Gilbert Roland *(Victor "Gaucho" Ribera),* Leo G. Carroll *(Henry Whitfield),* Vanessa Brown *(Kay Amiel),* Paul Stewart *(Syd Murphy),* Ivan Triesault *(Von Ellstein),* Elaine Stewart *(Lila),* Sammy White *(Gus),* Kathleen Freeman *(Miss March),* Marietta Canty *(Ida),* Robert Burton *(McDill).*

One of the peculiarities of Hollywood is that whenever it makes a film about Hollywood, the viewpoint is harsh and punishing. Movies are painfully hard to make and in making movies about themselves, the producers and their companies seem all too willing to pound their heads and air their dirty laundry. The studios are shown as being run by hard, ruthless men—as they are—and the people who work in them are depicted as ambitious, conniving, deceitful, power-hungry and sometimes larcenous. The indictment is overwhelming: *A Star Is Born* (1937 and 1954), *Sunset Boulevard* (1950), *The Star* (1953), *The Barefoot Contessa* (1954), *The Big Knife* (1955), *The Goddess* (1958), *The Carpetbaggers* (1964), *Harlow* (1965), *Inside Daisy Clover* (1966), and *The Oscar* (1967). From seeing these pictures no one should be encouraged to follow a career in the motion picture business, although there is no discouraging those who are possessed of film ambitions, a point that is also brought out in these unflattering character studies. Among the very best films of this ilk is *The Bad and*

With Barry Sullivan

the Beautiful, with Kirk Douglas playing a hard-driving producer who walks over everyone, and uses everyone, on his path to success. The characterization is a composite of actual Hollywood figures and it is said to be partly patterned after the careers of Val Lewton and David O. Selznick.

Jonathan Shields (Douglas) is a greatly talented but unpopular son of a film pioneer of similar character. At the funeral of his father, Jonathan is seen handing out money to various men in attendance—he has hired extras to appear as mourners. Down on his luck, Jonathan tries to get together some of the people whose careers he had built and whose success helped him become one of Hollywood's top producers. None of the ex-friends are interested in rushing back into his fold, and in a series of flashbacks the film tells why.

Early in his career the charming and facile Jonathan forms a partnership with a director, Fred Amiel (Barry Sullivan), and a producer, Harry Pebbel (Wal-

With Lana Turner

With Lana Turner

ter Pidgeon); together they work on film properties that eventually enable them to set up a studio. The director is a clever, artistic man but it is the astute drive and judgment of Jonathan that gives him the opportunity to realize his talents and become an established artist in Hollywood. Their association is long and fruitful, until the day Jonathan double-crosses him and assigns another director to handle one of Amiel's pictures. Since it was a film he par-

ticularly wanted to direct and one on which he had already done much work, Amiel walks out on Jonathan, vowing the partnership ended.

Georgia Lorrison (Lana Turner) is a young and beautiful, but depressed and alcoholic actress, who spends her time alone in her dingy apartment, idolizing her late actor-father. The walls are plastered with his photos and she listens to his recorded voice declaiming Shakespeare. The role is roughly based on

With Barry Sullivan, Lucille Know and Gilbert Roland

With Dick Powell

Diana Barrymore, and the John Barrymore-like voice on the recording belongs to Louis Calhern. Knowing her to be a woman of real talent, Jonathan visits her and taunts her into returning to her profession. He disparages her father and begs her not to be the personal failure he was—the tactic works and Georgia is soon putty in the knowing hands of Jonathan. He carefully coaches her and builds her into his biggest box-office star. She also falls in love with him, completely dependent on him and assuming that the love is returned. Jonathan appears loving but his commit-

ment is to his career and not a woman. When Georgia wins an award, she is hurt that Jonathan is not at the ceremony; then, rushing to his home to seek his congratulations, she finds him with a lovely, young actress (Elaine Stewart), all too clearly, and willingly, being geared for future stardom. Georgia is furious and she leaves Jonathan. However, she does not returning to drinking but continues her upward career as a movie star.

James Lee Bartlow (Dick Powell) is an affable college professor who writes a best selling novel that

With Barry Sullivan and Walter Pidgeon

With Lana Turner

is purchased by Jonathan and made into a successful film. Bartlow, comfortable in his hometown and not at all eager to leave and take up with Hollywood, is urged to do so by his young, lovey-dovey, social climbing southern belle of a wife, Rosemary (Gloria Grahame). Recognizing both Bartlow's talent as a writer and the glamour-hunger of his wife, Jonathan works on Rosemary, and the reluctant Bartlow is soon under contract to the Shields Studio. He, too, is molded by Jonathan into becoming a Hollywood success, but at the price of losing his wife. Jonathan sees Rosemary as a time wasting, interrupting force in her husband's life, and to get her out of the way he arranges an affair for her with a handsome Latin actor, Victor "Gaucho" Ribera (Gilbert Roland). Tragedy strikes when Rosemary and Victor are killed

With Lana Turner, Kathleen Freeman, Leo G. Carroll and Walter Pidgeon

in a plane crash; in consoling Bartlow, Jonathan trips on his own words and lets slip something that makes it obvious to the writer that Jonathan knew the couple were going away together. Bartlow smashes a fist into Jonathan's face, and another association ends.

The only partner who stays with Jonathan, and is not cheated by him, is his old production head, Harry Pebbel. Economy-minded and realistic, Harry does his best to keep the eager, ambitious, power-wheeling Jonathan on course. He advises and chastises but his counsel is never heeded. He has to stand by as Jonathan makes decisions that invite disaster, including firing a great director and taking over the directing of the epic himself, something Jonathan later concedes to be a great mistake. It is then Harry who calls in Fred Amiel, Georgia Lorrison and James Lee Bartlow to beg them to come back to Jonathan—pointing out that it was he who made them, as well as hurt them. All three decline, but as they leave the office they hear Harry talking on the phone to Jonathan. In the outer office, Georgia quietly picks up an extension and listens in on the conversation. Amiel and Bartlow crowd her to hear the voice, and as the film fades out we are left to think that the crafty, magnetic Jonathan might, perhaps, possibly get his old talent back.

The Bad and the Beautiful is a beautifully balanced piece of entertainment. Vincente Minnelli directed it with exact pacing, shading the scenes and developing the complicated stories and characters so that they neatly fitted into a fascinating jig-saw puzzle. Technically, the picture is perfection; the dialogue is compelling and the settings are particularly interesting to those who are curious about Hollywood studios and how they function. The music score by David Raksin is a masterpiece of its kind. The long statement of the main theme—a popular and oft recorded piece—was intended by the composer as a kind of siren-song, suggesting the lure of Jonathan and his glamorous business, and it performs precisely that function. The casting is almost beyond questioning: Pidgeon and Sullivan are exactly right as the producer and the director, and Dick Powell strikes the right key as the easy-going, tweedy, pipe smoking writer. Powell was originally cast to play the director but he asked Minnelli to let him do the writer. Lana Turner, then at the height of her glamorous appeal, clearly knew what she was about in limning a movie queen, and Gloria Grahame won an Oscar for her pretty but shrewd young wife. For Kirk Douglas it was a tour-de-force. The role of Jonathan Shields is one of the meatiest ever handed a Hollywood actor—not only as a subtle, dramatic vehicle but as an opportunity to reveal the character of the kind of film producer actors know but do not love.

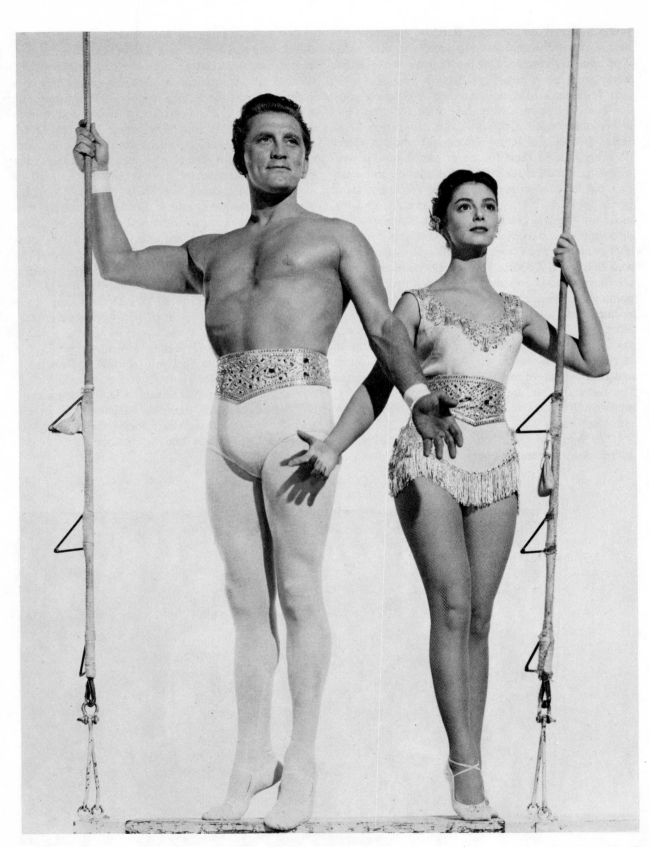

With Pier Angeli

With Richard Anderson

The Story of Three Loves

1953   An MGM Picture. *Produced by* Sidney Franklin. *Photographed in Technicolor by* Charles Rosher *and* Harold Rosson. *Edited by* Ralph E. Winters. *Musical score by* Miklos Rozsa. *Running time:* 122 minutes.

The Jealous Lover

1953   *Directed by* Gottfried Reinhardt. *Written by* John Collier.

CAST: James Mason *(Charles Coutray)*, Moira Shearer *(Paula Woodward)*, Agnes Moorehead *(Aunt Lydia)*.

Mademoiselle

1953   *Directed by* Vincente Minnelli. *Written by* Jan Lustig *and* George Froeschel. *Based on a story by* Arnold Phillips.

CAST: Ethel Barrymore *(Mrs. Pennicott)*, Leslie Caron *(Mademoiselle)*, Farley Granger *(Tommy)*, Ricky Nelson *(Tommy* [age 12]), Zsa Zsa Gabor *(Girl at Bar)*.

Equilibrium

1953   *Directed by* Gottfried Reinhardt. *Written by* John Collier; *adapted by* Jan Lustig *and* George Froeschel *from a story by* Ladislas Vajda.

CAST: Pier Angeli *(Nina)*, Kirk Douglas *(Pierre Narval)*, Richard Anderson *(Marcel)*.

The Story of Three Loves is precisely what its title implies. The trilogy of romances covers a wide assortment of sensations—tragic, whimsical and suspenseful. It is an MGM package of entertainment, slick and well contrived by masters of their trade.

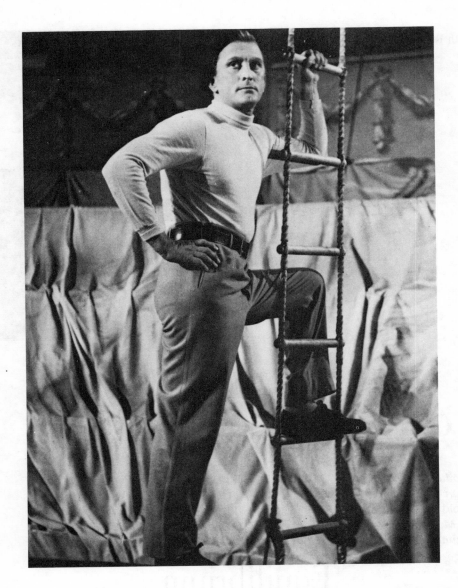

A team of art directors, headed by the estimable Cedric Gibbons, supplied beautiful settings; Frederick Ashton was brought in to do the choreography; and Miklos Rozsa composed a lush score, utilizing in one sequence Rachmaninoff's Paganini Variations, causing the work to become greatly popular. If *The Story of Three Loves* is formula movie entertainment, it is a formula that has been lost.

Each of the stories is told in flashback—always an effective device in relating romance. In the first, *The Jealous Lover,* James Mason appears as a ballet composer-impresario who falls in love with a lovely but frail dancer, beautifully played and danced by Moira Shearer. Because of her love for him she ignores medical advice and dances his ballet, bringing on the heart attack that ends her young life.

In the second story, *Mademoiselle,* Ethel Barrymore is a genial witch who grants the wish of a twelve-year-old boy that he suddenly become a grown man in order that he can escape the strict supervision of his governess. Since the governess is Leslie Caron and the boy turns into Farley Granger, romance is inevitable. The whimsy turns poignant when the wish runs its course after four hours and Leslie is left wondering where her lover has gone. But Barrymore promises a real love if the pretty governess will wait a year. Directed by Vincente Minnelli, *Mademoiselle* has charm and humor.

The most impressive episode of *The Story of Three Loves* is the last one, *Equilibrium,* with Kirk Douglas as a virile trapeze artist and Pier Angeli as a wistful girl he rescues from suicide and trains as his partner. The role required Douglas to perform trapeze stunts, and, as he had before with other roles requiring specific skills, he trained until he could actually perform the needed tricks. This part-film might well have been a full feature, it tells a good story and it is well paced with excitement and suspense. Douglas plays a famous circus performer who retires when his ambition to be the greatest practitioner of his art brings about the death of his partner. Known to be ruthlessly daring, he finds no trapeze girl willing to become his partner. But he does come across a sad little girl about to take her life because she believes herself guilty of unwittingly sending her husband to his death in a Nazi concentration camp. Douglas decides to make her his partner; the scenes showing him training her for the trapeze are tense and interesting, thanks to the direction of Gottfried Reinhardt. Assuming that her indifference to death will make her the perfect partner, Douglas coaches her to become a thrilling performer. What he does not reckon with is love. Angeli becomes so precious to him that after only one performance Douglas retires the act and gives up his ambition.

The staging of the trapeze sequences in *Equilibrium* are breathtaking, and the performances of Douglas and Angeli as two guilt-ridden people whose empty bitterness gradually softens into compassion and concern for one another makes it a memorable love story.

With Pier Angeli

With Pier Angeli

The Juggler

1953   A Stanley Kramer Company Production, *distributed by* Columbia Pictures. *Produced by* Stanley Kramer. *Directed by* Edward Dmytryk. *Written by* Michael Blankfort, *based on his novel. Photographed by* Roy Hunt. *Edited by* Aaron Stell. *Art director,* Robert Peterson. *Musical score by* George Antheil. *Running time:* 84 minutes.

CAST: Kirk Douglas *(Hans Muller),* Milly Vitale *(Ya'El),* Paul Stewart *(Detective Karni),* Joey Walsh *(Yehoshua Bresler),* Alf Kjellin *(Daniel),* Beverly Washburn *(Susy),* Charles Lane *(Rosenburg),* John Banner *(Emile Halevy),* Richard Benedict *(Kogan),* Oscar Karlweis *(Willy Schmidt),* John Bleifer *(Mordecai),* Greta Granstedt *(Carah),* Jay Adler *(Papa Sander),* Shep Menkin *(Dr. Traube),* Gabriel Curtiz *(Dr. Sklar).*

With Oscar Karlweis and Al Eben

The Juggler was one of several films Stanley Kramer produced for Columbia Pictures in 1952 and 1953. His contract called for him to make low-budget quality features. This Kramer did: *The Sniper, The Happy Time, Death of a Salesman, The Fourposter, The Member of the Wedding,* and this one with Kirk Douglas on location in Israel. All these films are admirable pieces of film craftsmanship, and all of them were disappointments at the box office. Columbia was not satisfied with the returns on these tasteful and intelligently unconventional pictures, and Kramer himself elected to become a director as well as a producer and pursue higher priced and more commercial subjects. Kramer, in hiring Douglas, clearly hoped to win from the public some of the acclaim given them for *Champion,* but the public did not respond with anything like the same fervor. This is a pity because *The Juggler* is in some ways a more interesting vehicle, far less obvious in its appeal, and containing a sensitive performance from Douglas as a

gentle but fear-tormented survivor of a Nazi concentration camp.

Michael Blankfort, who wrote the screenplay from his own novel, also acted as associate producer and was thus able to effect an accurate filming of his story. Kirk Douglas is Hans Muller, once a top-flight circus and vaudeville juggler but also a German Jew, who, like many others, had refused to believe the Nazis would move against their own citizens on the basis of creed. Muller has survived his years in the concentration camps but not so his wife and children. Bitter and neurotic, he arrives in Israel to find a new life. The impact of officialdom at the immigration camp has the frightened Muller running away on his first night there. In a Haifa waterfront café his suspicious manner causes a policeman (Richard Benedict) to follow him. Muller runs and is trapped in a courtyard. In his mind he imagines the Israeli cop to be a Nazi storm trooper, and he savagely knocks him down. Thinking he has killed the policeman, Muller panics with fear and runs off. But the scene is witnessed by a newspaperman (John Banner).

Muller leaves Haifa and spends the night in the rain on a park bench on Mount Carmel. In the morning, children find him and in his confusion he tells them he is an American tourist seeing Israel the cheap way. One of the boys, Yehoshua Bresler (Joey Walsh), is on his way to a kibbutz on the Syrian frontier and Muller offers to join him. His idea is that he will cross the frontier and make his way to Egypt to Jewish friends. Meanwhile, a detective (Paul Stewart) is assigned to track Muller down, following him through Jerusalem, to Nazareth, through modern housing developments and ruined Arab villages, and around the Sea of Galilee. As they travel, Muller amuses the boy with juggling tricks and stories, as much to allay his own anxiety as to amuse his companion. Approaching the kibbutz they stumble into a minefield and the boy is severely hurt in an explosion. As the boy is hospitalized, Muller is given a bed in a cottage normally occupied by a girl Ya'El (Milly Vitale), whose husband has been killed fighting the Arabs. After a while, gradually falling in love with the girl, Muller admits he is not an American tourist and that he is guilty of killing a policeman.

Finally, the detective appears at the kibbutz, just as Muller is delighting an audience of children with a juggling show. He makes them laugh by missing an egg and having it drop on his head, but his expression of disgust concerning the egg lying smashed on his head turns to fear as he spots the detective. He runs from the room, seizes a gun and sets about defending himself. The detective explains to Muller that the policeman is not dead, and that he will have to face

With Milly Vitale

With Milly Vitale

justice on the charge of assault. The sympathetic detective convinces Muller that he is among friends, telling him that he is himself a former refugee. With this and the love of the girl, Muller realizes that he is in need of psychiatric help, and that his future is safe in his new country.

The Juggler is a small gem of a film, sensibly directed by Edward Dmytryk, exactly photographed by Roy Hunt, and delicately scored by George An-

theil, who used several Jewish melodies to subtle advantage. The acting rings true, especially the excellent Paul Stewart as the detective, but it is Kirk Douglas' performance that gives the film its emotional impact. His Muller is a spiritually terrified man, haunted by hideous memories but trying to appear the self-assured entertainer who once was. It is a major piece of film acting.

Act of Love

1953   An Anatole Litvak Production, *distributed by* United Artists. *Produced and directed by* Anatole Litvak. *Written by* Irwin Shaw, *based on the novel* The Girl on the Via Flaminia *by* Alfred Hayes. *Photographed by* Armand Thirard. *Edited by* William Hornbeck. *Musical score by* Michel Emer *and* Joe Hajos. *Running time:* 108 minutes.

CAST: Kirk Douglas *(Robert Teller),* Dany Robin *(Lisa),* Barbara Laage *(Nina),* Robert Strauss *(Blackwood),* Gabrielle Dorziat *(Adele),* Gregoire Aslan *(Commissaire),* Martha Mercadier *(Young Woman),* Fernand Ledoux *(Fernand),* Serge Reggiani *(Claude),* Brigitte Bardot *(Mimi),* Gilbert Geniat *(Mme. Hen-* derson), George Mathews *(Henderson),* Leslie Dwyer *(English Sergeant),* Richard Benedict *(Pete).*

In making a film based on Alfred Hayes' novel, *The Girl on the Via Flaminia,* Anatole Litvak decided to switch the locale from the Roman capital to the French, causing a number of changes, especially the title, that may have impaired the original story. Filmed entirely in France, *Act of Love* is thoroughly Litvak; he produced and directed the picture, co-scripted the screenplay with Irwin Shaw and financed it. The Russian-born Litvak is one of the cinema's great stylists; making films in Russia, Germany and France before the Second World War, working in Hollywood from 1937 to 1950, and then returning to Europe. Litvak

With Dany Robin

has a penchant for the tender and the tragic—*Mayerling* (1936), *All This, and Heaven Too* (1940), *This Above All* (1942), *The Snake Pit* (1949), *Anastasia* (1956)—and *Act of Love* is very much of this genre. Most critics have found the film overlong, and Litvak admits that "it didn't work out as well as I thought it would, some of which was my own fault."

Act of Love is told mostly as a flashback. Robert Teller (Kirk Douglas) is an American who visits the French Riviera some years after the war. He wanders around the town of Villefranche as he waits for his hotel room to be made up, then he sits by the dockside and suns himself, as his mind relives the sad experience of a decade earlier. Now it is Paris, 1944, shortly after the Liberation; Teller is a GI assigned to duty as a clerk. He meets a waif-like French girl named Lisa and finds her to be hungry and homeless. Teller is looking for accommodation in the city and he realizes he has a better chance of finding a room as a married man than as a single man. He persuades Lisa to agree to the ruse of pretending to be married. Once settled, problems arise when the girl is unable

With Dany Robin

With Robert Strauss

to show identification papers and a marriage certificate, and she is then officially listed by the police as a prostitute.

Teller is soon deeply in love with the gentle, wistful girl. Life takes on new meaning for them and they enjoy themselves with friends in Paris. Teller goes to his commanding officer (George Mathews) and asks for permission to marry. The CO, trying to be understanding, explains that he is swamped with requests from GI's wanting to marry European girls and that he thinks most of these lonely, infatuated men are making a mistake. Teller pleads his case but the CO becomes adamant and denies permission. The news crushes the spirit of the emotionally fragile girl, and as Teller scurries around Paris trying to think of other ways of getting a license, Lisa is last seen sadly looking into the Seine River.

Back in Villefranche, Teller's daydreaming is disturbed by a fellow American tourist. The man turns out to be his ex-commanding officer. He reminds

With Dany Robin

Teller of the wartime romance and how he saved him from what would probably have been a disastrous marriage. He then asks Teller if he knows whatever happened to the girl. With quiet bitterness Teller replies, "They found her in the river—a long time ago."

Kirk Douglas and Dany Robin carry the Litvak film with their excellent playing of the luckless couple. Douglas is particularly good in those scenes when his anxiety runs cross-current with his tenderness for the girl. Gruff Robert Strauss is fine as a sergeant who tries to help Douglas forge a marriage permit, and George Mathews is just right as the officer who believes that what he is doing is for the best. Most of the cast is made up of expert French players, although their accents tend to cloud the effectiveness for American ears. Brigitte Bardot appears in a small role, early in her career. For the most part, *Act of Love* is too leisurely in its pace, but it does convey the tenor of life in Paris in the confused days after the Liberation. It also has mood and atmosphere and proves again that few film makers can tell a poignant tale better than Litvak.

Ulysses

1954   A Lux Film, *distributed by* Paramount. *Produced by* Dino De Laurentiis *and* Carlo Ponti, *in association with* William Schorr. *Directed by* Mario Camerini. *Screenplay by* Franco Brusati, Mario Camerini, Ennio de Concini, Hugh Gray, Ben Hecht, Ivo Perilli *and* Irwin Shaw, *based on* Homer's *Odyssey.* *Photographed by* Harold Rosson. *Art director,* Flavio Mogherini. *Edited by* Leo Cattozzo. *Musical score by* Alessandro Cicognini. *Running time:* 104 minutes.

CAST: Kirk Douglas *(Ulysses),* Silvana Mangano *(Penelope and Circe),* Anthony Quinn *(Antinous),* Rossana Podesta *(Nausicca),* Sylvie *(Euriclea),* Daniel Ivernel *(Euriloco),* Jacques Dumesnil *(Alcinous).*

Ulysses is one of the many films that might be described as impressive failures. Admirable in its attempts to translate episodes of Homer's *Odyssey* into a lusty adventure yarn, the picture fails to make its fantasy believable. Kirk Douglas plays the Greek super-hero with brawn and vitality but he all too obviously looks like an American actor cast in an Italian picture. Anthony Quinn also appears but it is a small and unimportant part and he is completely wasted. The style of both Douglas and Quinn is at variance with their Italian co-workers, especially in the English soundtrack version, where the dubbing sabotages the production. Of interest are the spacious sets built at the Ponti-De Laurentiis Studios in Rome and the Mediterranean locations, which the producers claim are those described by Homer.

Seven writers worked on the script of *Ulysses,* among them Ben Hecht and Irwin Shaw. It might have been better had the script been the work of just one, but it nonetheless does a fair job of synthesizing the vast *Odyssey.* In this respect the film is of especial interest to students of Greek mythology. Basically it is the story of a man who took a long time to get home to Greece after fighting in the Trojan War. It tells how the palace of the lovely Penelope of Ithaca is invaded by a number of powerful and insolent

suitors who propose that she marry one of them. Her heroic husband Ulysses (Douglas) has been gone ten years, involved in the Trojan War, and they believe he will never return. The faithful Penelope believes otherwise. Ulysses is now seen as the captain of the soldiers inside the huge wooden horse that was towed into Troy by its curious citizens. Ulysses and his men sack the city and head for home. When next we see him he is lying unconscious on an island shore, a victim of a shipwreck and also the victim of amnesia.

A beautiful young princess (Rossana Podesta) discovers Ulysses and he is welcomed and cared for as a guest. She falls in love with him, especially after seeing him best a wrestling champion in a public exhibition, and marriage seems inevitable. But Ulysses is a troubled man and he spends much time at the shore peering out to sea and trying to remember the past. The film fills in the gaps with flashbacks: he recalls the great storm that destroyed his ship and how he and his men found themselves in the land of

With Silvana Mangano

the Cyclops, a one-eyed, murderous giant, and how they escaped from his cave by getting him drunk and running a battering ram into his eye.

Ulysses remembers sailing past the coast of the sirens, whose songs lure sailors to their death. Plugging the ears of his men with wax, he has himself lashed to the mast with ropes so that he can hear the call. What he hears causes him to try to break loose from his bindings—what he hears is the voice of his wife begging him to return. According to Homer, each man hears what he most wants to hear. Next Ulysses and his men arrive on the island of Circe the Enchantress, who takes on the appearance of Penelope. Both roles are played by Silvana Mangano, exotic in her beauty but rather wooden in her performance. She tries but fails to keep him in her company.

After much reminiscing on the beach Ulysses' mind is cleared and he announces his identity to his hosts and to his distraught fiancée. They provide him with a ship and he returns home, entering his kingdom dressed as a beggar. Unrecognized he visits his house and finds it full of suitors, now carousing in their confidence that Penelope will marry one of them. They humiliate the beggar but his revenge is almost immediate. The suitors challenge one another—he who can bend the bow of Ulysses will be the bridegroom. None can bend the mighty bow, except the beggar, who then drops his disguise and rapidly liquidates each and every one of the suitors, including Anthony Quinn. After years of loneliness and constancy Penelope is rewarded by the return of her hero.

Ulysses is far beyond the ludicrous standard of most Italian film epics dealing with ancient times. Kirk Douglas chose to play the part respectfully, giving the role of the semi-barbaric Greek king moments of sensitivity and thoughtfulness. Douglas could easily

have hammed the part and played it as a romp. He wisely avoided this, his Ulysses is a puzzled, wandering man with more than a little wit and dignity. Unfortunately no other character in the picture is allowed by the script or by the direction to match the leading role. Hence the Ulysses of this film is as lonely as he is lost.

20,000 Leagues Under the Sea

1954   A Walt Disney Production, *distributed by* Buena Vista. *Directed by* Richard Fleischer. *Written by* Earl Fenton, *based on the book by* Jules Verne. *Photographed in Technicolor by* Franz Planer. *Special effects photography by* Ralph Hammeras. *Edited by* Elmo Williams. *Art director,* John Meehan.

Musical score by Paul Smith. *Running time:* 120 minutes.

CAST: Kirk Douglas *(Ned Land)*, James Mason *(Captain Nemo)*, Paul Lukas *(Professor Aronnax)*, Peter Lorre *(Conseil)*, Robert J.

With Peter Lorre and Paul Lukas

With Peter Lorre

Wilke *(Mate on "Nautilus")*, Carleton Young *(John Howard)*, Ted de Corsia *(Captain Farragut)*, Percy Helton *(Diver)*, Ted Cooper *(Mate on "Lincoln")*, Edward Marr *(Shipping Agent)*, Fred Graham *(Casey Moore)*, J. M. Kerrigan *(Billy)*.

Jules Verne published his book *20,000 Leagues Under the Sea* in 1870 and startled his readers with a story about a weird and wonderful submersible ship that explored the mysteries of the ocean depths, com-

With Peter Lorre and Paul Lukas

manded by a strange genius of a man called Nemo. The great science-fiction writer was years ahead of his time—no submarines were then operable and few knew anything of oceanography. It was an epic piece of literature, and Walt Disney's screen treatment is an epic visualization. The shrewd Disney, the most consistently successful of all film producers, poured more than five million dollars into this, his first live-action picture, produced in his Burbank studio, and it was a solid investment. The film is photographically ingenious and exciting, the story is fascinating, the acting is faultless. At one point, Kirk Douglas, playing a lusty, roguish sailor, sings a chantey titled "A Whale of a Tale," and it neatly sums up the whole enterprise.

In his fine screenplay, Earl Fenton preserved the spirit of the original and managed to condense the elaborate story, making it fit the framework of a two-hour telling. He was, of course, vastly aided by the great talents and resources of the Disney Special Effects and Processes Department. The story begins in 1868, as news of an awesome, monstrous and aggressive "thing" sweeps the nautical world. Tales of vessels being swiftly destroyed by this apparition reach the U.S. Government and an armed frigate is sent to find and destroy the mysterious craft. Instead, the monster sinks the frigate, and three survivors—Ned Land, a harpoonist (Douglas), Professor Pierre Aronnax (Paul Lucas), a distinguished authority on undersea life, and Conseil, his assistant (Peter Lorre)—find themselves on board a submarine. They also find that their hosts, Captain Nemo (James Mason) and his crew, are world-haters, dedicated to destroying all they can. However, their evil genius, especially that of their cultured captain, demands respect. The submarine, the Nautilus, is operated by atomic power,

With Peter Lorre and James Mason

and equipped with electrical and mechanical wonders. In their involuntary roles as prisoner-guests, the trio makes a trip around the world, observing at first hand the marvels of the deep.

Although Aronnax and Conseil would be content to stay aboard and learn more of Nemo's science and inventions, the plebian Ned is anxious to escape. He tries once when the submarine stops at a lonely island, but savage cannibals chase him back to the comparative safety of the Nautilus. Seizing every opportunity, he inserts notes containing the location of Nemo's secret island, Vulcania, in bottles and tosses them hopefully into the ocean. Shelled by a lone warship, the Nautilus sinks thousands of feet into the ocean before Nemo and his men can repair a broken shaft and regain control. While they are deeper than man has ever before ventured, they observe the strange and magical wonderland of life miles down in the sea. As they head for Vulcania, the submarine is attacked by two giant squids. Ned saves Nemo's life after he has been grasped by a huge tentacle. Now softer in his attitude, Nemo reveals his plans to use his three prisoners as emissaries to negotiate a peace with the outside world. But enemy warships await them in the harbor of Vulcania—Ned's bottles have been found. Determined not to share his secrets, Nemo gets ashore and sets a time bomb. He is fatally wounded on his trip back to the submarine but before he dies he orders a straight-down course for the last voyage of the Nautilus. Ned eludes his guards and manages to flee the vessel, along with Aronnax and Conseil. Later they watch in fascination as the enormous bomb goes off, obliterating the island, the warships, the Nautilus, and the secrets of Nemo. They muse about some future time when man may know

With Peter Lorre

how to use such inventiveness and such violent force for more reasonable and intelligent purposes.

20,000 Leagues Under the Sea is, as it deserves to be, a greatly successful film. For Kirk Douglas it gives him ample scope to rolic as a roguish adventurer, and for James Mason it is yet another opportunity to reveal his talent for creating villains of unusual depth-of-character and culture. But the real stars of the film are the men who created the fantastic sets and special effects, in particular art director John Meehan, and Ub Iwerks, Disney's Special Processes genius. The biggest single production problem was the creation of the Nautilus; Verne made things difficult for Disney by requiring the vessel to be something resembling a sea monster—so that Nemo's enemies would not know they were being attacked by a man-made machine. According to Verne, the Nautilus had a battering-ram snout, electric eyes, a series of metallic ridges along its spine, and an enormous tail. When the Disney workers had completed their craft, it was 200 feet long and 22 feet at its widest point. It also, true to Verne, had a main lounge with a pipe organ, a library, rare paintings, plush, ornate furniture and aquariums full of unusual fish.

The many underwater sequences called for the building of a huge tank at the Disney studio. The company went on location to Jamaica for the cannibal island sequence, and the extensive diving footage was done in the crystal-clear waters of the Bahamas, off Nassau. The time, effort and skill put into the making of *20,000 Leagues Under the Sea* are all handsomely apparent; it is an entertaining and admirable piece of film making.

With James Mason, Peter Lorre and Paul Lukas

[117]

The Racers

1955   A 20th Century-Fox Film. *Produced by* Julian Blaustein. *Directed by* Henry Hathaway. *Written by* Charles Kaufman, *based on the novel by* Hans Ruesch. *Photographed in Deluxe Color by* Joe MacDonald. *Edited by* James B. Clark. *Art directors,* Lyle Wheeler *and* George Patrick. *Musical score by* Alex North. *Running time:* 112 minutes.

CAST: Kirk Douglas *(Gino)*, Bella Darvi *(Nicole)*, Gilbert Roland *(Dell 'Oro)*, Cesar Romero *(Carlos)*, Lee J. Cobb *(Maglio)*, Katy Jurado *(Maria)*, Charles Goldner *(Piero)*, John Hudson *(Michel Caron)*, George Dolenz *(Count Salem)*, Agnes Laury *(Toni)*, John Wengraf *(Dr. Tabor)*, Richard Allan *(Pilar)*, Francesco de Scaffa *(Chata)*, Norman Schiller *(Dehlgren)*, Mel Welles *(Fiori)*, Gene D'Arcy *(Rousillon)*, Mike Dengate *(Dell 'Oro's Mechanic)*, Peter Brocco *(Gatti)*, Stephen Bekassy *(Race Official)*.

The Racers bears comparison with *Champion*, although it is not as vital or as dramatically sound as the former film. Both deal with a man determined to raise himself from the lower level of society and attain the wealth and respect that come with being a sports celebrity. It is the kind of man most understood by Kirk Douglas. In *The Racers* he is an Italian bus driver with a burning ambition to crack the world of sports car racing, and we see him first entering the Grand Prix de Napoli with his home-built car, competing against some of the best drivers and best machines in the business. From there his ambition takes him through the famed runways of Europe; his adventures, triumphs and mishaps giving the audience an insight into the life style and psyche of racing drivers.

Briskly directed by Henry Hathaway and finely photographed in Deluxe Color by Joe MacDonald, *The Racers* is at its best when the wheels are spinning fast; like many another film dealing with sport, it suffers from a banal story and dubious characterizations. It tries to augment its appeal to feminine au-

With Bella Darvi

diences by having its heroine a ballet dancer, one interested in high fashion. Thus female viewers glimpse the insides of fashion salons, in addition to scenic shots of the French Riviera, Paris, Rome, and the authentic locations of famed auto racing sites. But again, it is the plot that hangs heavy.

The late Bella Darvi appears as the lovely ballerina, who takes the eye of Douglas when she visits the Neapolitan racing event. They fall in love and she becomes his mistress, dutifully following him as he progresses in his ambition. He warns her of the heartaches that will be involved if she ties her life to his, but she cannot be dissuaded. Indeed, she buys him a racing car and sets him up—and off. He almost immediately wins the Mille Miglia, and enters the company of champions, two of whom are played by Gilbert Roland and Cesar Romero. Douglas follows the circuit but finds his luck inconsistent, and occa-

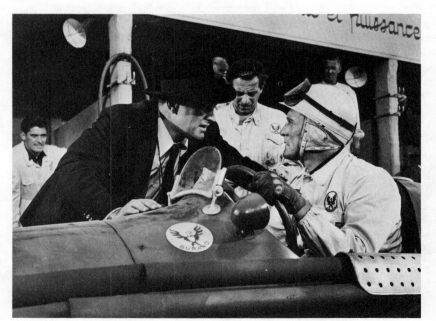

With Lee J. Cobb and Charles Goldner

With Bella Darvi

sionally painful. He is badly injured in the Swiss Grand Prix and comes close to having a leg amputated in a hospital. Still doggedly determined, he hobbles on crutches for an impatient year but regains his strength and re-enters the business as a co-driver to Roland in the Le Mans race. When Roland gets accidentally burned at a pit stop, Douglas finishes the race alone and wins it. He continues to win races until he stands fourth in world's competition.

The hero of *The Racers* becomes a man obsessed with ambition; his injuries cause him to take drugs to ward off pain, and he also becomes unethical in his

With Charles Goldner

fierce competitiveness, thereby losing the affection and esteem of his colleagues. Eventually, he loses his mistress, who prefers to return to the ballet. His career slows down, he becomes dispirited and wanders away from the business. One day he meets an old racing friend in Paris, who tells him Darvi is still in love with him. Douglas then follows the ballet trail and locates the girl, but she is reluctant to take up with him again. Invited to take part in the Grand Prix d'Italia, Douglas sacrifices his chance to win by saving the life of his competing friend Roland. At a pit stop he spots Darvi in the stands—she waves at him as he gets back into his car to finish a race he knows he can't possibly win. He smiles, and we assume that the bitterness and the ruthlessness have left him, and that in reformation he will find his happiness with his girl.

There are some exceptional racing shots in *The Racers* and the film remains an item of interest to car buffs, even though the impact has been lessened by the more recent and more incisive racing films like *Grand Prix* and *Le Mans*. The strain of the story line is also made bearable by a few interesting performances; for Douglas the film required little new in his acting of a challenger beyond acquiring greater knowledge about the art of driving, which he was keen to do. For Bella Darvi *The Racers* was yet one more vain attempt to find stardom, but Lee J. Cobb shines as a racing manager, Charles Goldner as Douglas' mechanic-companion and the veteran Gilbert Roland as a knight of the speedways.

With Bella Darvi

With Lee J. Cobb, Charles Goldner and Bella Darvi

With Jeanne Crain

Man Without a Star

1955   A Universal Picture. *Produced by* Aaron Rosenberg. *Directed by* King Vidor. *Written by* Borden Chase *and* D. D. Beauchamp, *based on the novel by* Dee Linford. *Photographed in Technicolor by* Russell Metty. *Edited by* Virgil Vogel. *Art directors,* Alexander Golitzen *and* Richard H. Riedel. *Musical supervision by* Joseph Gershenson. *Running time:* 89 minutes.

CAST: Kirk Douglas *(Dempsey Rae),* Jeanne Crain *(Reed Bowman),* Claire Trevor *(Idonee),* William Campbell *(Jeff Jimson),* Richard Boone *(Steve Miles),* Jay C. Flippen *(Strap Davis),* Myrna Hansen *(Tess Cassidy),* Mara Corday *(Moccasin Mary),* Eddy C. Waller *(Tom Cassidy),* Sheb Wooley *(Latigo),* George Wallace *(Tom Carter),* Frank Chase *(Little Waco),* Paul Birch *(Mark Tolliver),* Roy Barcroft *(Sheriff Olson),* William "Bill" Phillips *(Cookie).*

The Kirk Douglas of *Man Without a Star* is a different man from the one who rode *Along the Great Divide.* Only four years separate the two films but whereas Douglas tended to look like an easterner on an outing in the previous picture, he here seems like a western rogue to the saddle born. *Man Without a Star* is an amusing, lively little horse-opera and Douglas is perfect as an easy-going cowpoke, not too fond of work but with an eye for the ladies and a fancy way with six-shooters. Director King Vidor had long established his ability with action sequences and pictorial scope in films like *Northwest Passage* (1940), and *Duel in the Sun* (1947), and *Man Without a Star* has a full measure of Vidor directed barroom fights, stampedes and chases.

The theme of the film is the gradual disappearance of freedom as the Wild West settles down to business and puts up barbed wire to mark the lines of investment. Dempsey Rae (Douglas) is a happy wanderer, content to move further and further west to escape the fences. He meets up with a naïve farmboy, Jeff Jimson (William Campbell), who yearns to

With William Campbell and Jeanne Crain

be a gun-totin' cowboy. In Dempsey he finds the right tutor. The two team up and rove together, as Dempsey shows the young lad some fancy tricks in spinning six-guns and in the art of the fast draw. He also fills him in on the lore and the codes of the West, including such information as, "a stranger doesn't dismount before a ranch house until he's invited to step down." Since the script is partly the work of Borden Chase, the information can be considered sound.

The two chums get themselves a job working for a beautiful ranch owner, Reed Bowman (Jeanne Crain), who turns out to be as unscrupulous as she is handsome. Reed is the kind of lady who installs a new-fangled inside bathroom—something from which her rough workers derive some crude humor—and the kind of rancher willing to ride down the fences of her neighbors and hog the whole range. Dempsey is happy to work for the lady for $30 a month and even happier to make love to her but he draws the

With William Campbell

With Claire Trevor and William Campbell

line at laying down his life for her in range wars. He quits the crooked beauty and drifts into the nearby town, to renew his acquaintance with Idonee (Claire Trevor), a madam with the proverbial heart of gold. The devil-may-care lad announces his presence in her establishment by throwing his saddle in the window. He also combs his hair with water from a goldfish bowl, and accompanies himself on the banjo as he sings a saucy ballad called "And the Moon Grew Brighter and Brighter."

The likable Dempsey is rocked out of his contentment by his successor at the Bowman Ranch, a brute named Steve Miles (Richard Boone) who feels he has to lick every man in sight, especially when enticed by

With Richard Boone and William Campbell

With Richard Boone

his glamorous employer. Miles and his men attack Dempsey in the street and savagely beat him. It is then that Dempsey stops being affable and becomes aggressive, leading the local ranchers in a campaign to halt the ambitions of the powerful lady rancher.

Man Without a Star offers little plot in its briskly paced hour-and-a-half running time, but it has more than its share of humor. The incidents and the characters make it an entertaining item, especially Kirk Douglas in his expertise with guns and horses. Obvi-

ously the result of much time and effort, he leaps onto horses like a gymnast and indulges in some elaborate pistol twirling. Douglas also learned how to play the banjo, to back up his fairly good warbling of a song. His Dempsey Rae is a vagabond who, at the end of the story, drifts off into a hazy future. The slightly sad moral of the film, exemplified by its title, is that everyone must have a star to keep them steadfast, and that those who don't are doomed to wander.

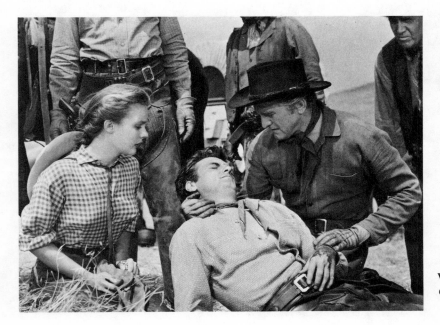

With Myrna Hansen and William Campbell

With Harry Landers

The Indian Fighter

With Elsa Martinelli

1955   A Bryna Production, *distributed by* United Artists. *Produced by* William Schorr. *Directed by* Andre de Toth. *Written by* Frank Davis *and* Ben Hecht, *based on a story by* Ben Kadish. *Photographed in Technicolor by* Wilfrid M. Cline. *Edited by* Richard Cahoon. *Art director,* Wiard Ihnen. *Musical score by* Franz Waxman. *Running time:* 88 minutes.

CAST: Kirk Douglas *(Johnny Hawks)*, Elsa Martinelli *(Onahti)*, Walter Abel *(Captain Trask)*, Walter Matthau *(Wes Todd)*, Diana Douglas *(Susan Rogers)*, Eduard Franz *(Red Cloud)*, Lon Chaney *(Chivington)*, Alan Hale *(Will Crabtree)*, Elisha Cook *(Briggs)*, Michael Winkelman *(Tommy Rogers)*, Harry Landers *(Grey Wolf)*, William Phipps *(Lt. Blake)*, Buzz Henry *(Lt. Shaeffer)*, Ray Teal *(Morgan)*, Frank Cady *(Trader Joe)*, Hank Worden *(Crazy Bear)*, Lane Chandler *(Head Settler)*.

With Eduard Franz

For the first production of his own film company, Bryna, Kirk Douglas wisely chose a western and one with above average scenic values. Filmed in Oregon, *The Indian Fighter* is a frontier adventure yarn, with no cowboys but a great many Indians who are revealed in a more interesting light than they had previously been shown on screen. These are Indians with family lives, and some strategical sense of warfare.

The film also broke new ground by giving Indians a little sex appeal. Douglas, as a lusty frontier scout, ogles the lovely Indian maiden Onahti—played by Italian actress Elsa Martinelli in her first American film—as she bathes in a pool, and later when they become lovers they are seen frolicking nude in the waters together. It's a refreshing and titilating new insight into old frontier life.

With Walter Matthau

With Diana Douglas

The Indian Fighter concerns the efforts of a wagon train heading for Oregon in 1870. The train halts at a small, unmanned frontier fort when the Sioux will not let them pass through their territory, and a seasoned scout and Indian expert, Johnny Hawks (Douglas), is assigned by the army to aid them. Hawks straightaway goes to the camp of the dignified Chief Red Cloud (Eduard Franz) who explains that the trouble was started by white whisky traders, trying to fleece the Indians of their gold. Hawks promises to settle the situation and the Chief agrees to appear at the fort to sign a peace treaty. However, his pugnacious brother Grey Wolf (Harry Landers) repudiates peace talk because he despises all white men as dishonorable. The Chief's daughter Onahti is also miffed at Hawks for peeping at her

during her bathing, but being very female she is nonetheless somewhat intrigued by the humorous, healthy Hawks.

That night, an Indian is murdered and Grey Wolf captures Wes Todd (Walter Matthau). Hawks challenges the Indian for possession of the white man; they fight Sioux-style, mounted and with knives, and Hawks gets the better of the Indian, but he refuses to kill him. Hawks then tells Red Cloud he will take Todd to Fort Laramie to be tried. En route, Todd puts the blame for the killing on his partner, Chivington (Lon Chaney) and tries to win the friendship of the scout. At the fort, Hawks reports to the commandant (Walter Abel), who jails both Todd and Chivington. Red Cloud and his chieftains arrive at the fort and the treaty is signed. Meanwhile, Hawks becomes a great favorite of a young boy (Michael Winkleman) and his widowed, husband-hungry mother (Diana Douglas, ex-wife of Kirk), but the free-wheeling scout is not a man to be pinned down.

Hawks is given the job of guide and guard to the wagon train, and the large party resumes its quest westward. Todd and Chivington, released from jail, dog the wagon train because they feel Hawks will again dally with the Indians and possibly lead them to gold—they assume the Indians have a mine. The villains know their man. Hawks takes the wagon train off its course, into Indian country, because he wants to see Onahti. While he is with her, Indians come to the settlers to trade. Todd and Chivington get an Indian drunk and just as he is revealing the source of the gold, the furious Grey Wolf bursts on the scene. In the ensuing fight, Grey Wolf and several others are killed, and the settlers head back for the fort.

Following the panic stricken wagon train back to the fort, Hawks is almost lynched by the scared settlers, who claim he deserted them. But when the fort is attacked by Indians, the settlers know they need Hawks. He calmly instructs them in defense methods, to ward off the methodically attacking braves—the Indians use long saplings as catapults, whisking bales of fire at the fort. Under cover of darkness, Hawks slips out and goes to see Onahti. She takes him to the Indian gold mine where, as he guessed, Todd and Chivington are busy working. Todd sets off an explosion to get away—the holocaust kills Chivington but Hawks manages to get Todd and take him back to the Indian camp. Red Cloud is poised for his final assault on the fort; Hawks and Onahti explain the situation, including the news that they want to get married, and the Indian Chief relents on both issues—martial and marital. In the final scenes, the wagon train winds its happy way through the hills as the two lovers romp in the pool.

The Indian Fighter is a lively item, thanks to director Andre de Toth, who keeps the familiar story line moving at a fair clip. Whenever he shows the wagon train, it is galloping and not plodding. The material is trite but the production values give it gloss, and the film benefits greatly from its applied research on Indian life. Douglas' portrait of Hawks is suitably vigorous and possibly comes close to depicting the

With Walter Matthau and Lon Chaney

actual character of such a man—a self-confidant, work-for-a-price rogue. Certainly, in his bareback pony riding and his Indian wrestling, Douglas was in top-notch physical form.

With Eduard Franz

Lust for Life

1956   An MGM Picture. *Produced by* John Houseman. *Directed by* Vincente Minnelli. *Written by* Norman Corwin, *based on the novel by* Irving Stone. *Photographed in* MetroColor *by* F. A. Young *and* Russell Harlan. *Edited by* Adrienne Fazan. *Art directors,* Cedric Gibbons, Hans Peters, *and* Preston Ames. *Musical score by* Miklos Rozsa. *Running time:* 122 minutes.

CAST: Kirk Douglas (*Vincent Van Gogh*), Anthony Quinn (*Paul Gauguin*), James Donald (*Theo Van Gogh*), Pamela Brown (*Christine*), Everett Sloan (*Dr. Gachet*), Niall MacGinnis (*Roulin*), Noel Purcell (*Anton Mauve*), Henry Daniell (*Theodorus Van Gogh*), Madge Kennedy (*Anna Cornelia Van Gogh*), Jill Bennett (*Willemien*), Lionel Jeffries (*Dr. Peyron*), Laurence Naismith (*Dr. Bosman*), Eric Pohlmann (*Colbert*), Jeanette Sterke (*Kay*), Toni Gerry (*Johanna*), Wilton Graff (*Rev. Stricker*), Isobel Elson (*Mrs. Stricker*),

David Horne (*Rev. Peters*), Noel Howlett (*Commissioner Van Den Berghe*), Ronald Adams (*Commissioner De Smet*), John Ruddock (*Ducrucq*), Julie Robinson (*Rachel*), David Leonard (*Camille Pissarro*), William Phipps (*Emile Bernard*), David Bond (*Seurat*), Frank Peris (*Pere Tanguy*), Jay Adler (*Waiter*), Laurence Badie (*Adeline Ravoux*).

That a Hollywood studio in the mid-1950's should proceed to make a film about a great painter was in itself surprising, but that the end result should be an artistic and cultural achievement is amazing. The project was completely atypical. Yet *Lust for Life* is a beautiful and faithful account of the life of Vincent Van Gogh, and manages to convey his genius and his personal agony. A quick scanning of the film's credits explains its quality; producer John Houseman, the man who helped Orson Welles establish the famed Mercury Theatre; Vincente Minnelli, a director of taste and sensitivity; color photography by Freddy Young and Russell Harlan; a musical score by Miklos Rozsa;

With Jeanette Sterke

With Pamela Brown

a script by Norman Corwin; and a team of art directors headed by Cedric Gibbons. But no matter how impressive the talents behind the camera, *Lust for Life* was a film whose success would have to hang on the actor who played Van Gogh—and from Kirk Douglas it received an astonishing performance. Greatly in his favor was a resemblance to the painter, and as Minnelli recalls, "Once we received the green light to proceed with the picture, there was no question that Kirk would play Van Gogh. No other actor was even considered for the part."

With MGM money and, in this instance, good judgment, Houseman and Minnelli were able to make the film exactly as they wished. They went on location in France in the summer of 1955 and managed to do most of their filming in the actual places Van Gogh lived and worked. In a few remarkable sequences, they duplicated the scenes of several Van Gogh landscapes; photographers Young and Harlan beautifully juxtaposed stunning frames with the paintings. The Dutch interiors early in the film have a subtlety of light and shadow that suggest Rembrandt, and the photographers' pastoral scenes indicate that Van Gogh must have been influenced by Millet. With the co-operation of various museums and private collectors Houseman had access to some two hundred Van Gogh originals, which he had Young and Harlan photograph in color and incorporate into the film.

With Anthony Quinn

Van Gogh did not set out with the idea of being a painter. *Lust for Life* begins in 1878 when the intense young Dutchman arrives in the Belgian coal-mining district of Le Borinage intent on bringing them religious instruction and spiritual aid. His desire to serve and his sympathy for the poor miners and

their families causes him to give them everything he has. This unrestrained zeal, typical of Van Gogh's fanatical approach to every situation, brings him into conflict with his superiors, who feel his behavior degrades the church. He refuses to change, and disgusted with their apparent lack of compassion, he quits his evangelical calling. This sends him into a period of depression; when his brother Theo (James Donald) arrives in Le Borinage he finds Van Gogh living in squalor. Theo persuades him to return to their comfortable middle-class home in Holland, at least to recover his health. At home, Van Gogh starts to pursue a dawning interest in art; a passionate man by nature, he feels the need to express love and he impulsively proposes to a cousin, who violently rejects him.

In The Hague, Van Gogh takes up with a prostitute (Pamela Brown) who becomes his housekeeper and his model as he strives to master the techniques of painting. A relative, painter Anton Mauve (Noel Purcell), offers to help, and does, but Van Gogh is a man who cannot defer to anyone and he soon loses the friendship of Mauve. He returns to the family home in Nuenen when his father dies; some time later he is asked by his sister to leave the house because of the ridicule his eccentric behavior is bringing on the family. Van Gogh goes from there to Paris to live with his brother Theo, seemingly the one person in the world who loves, understands and encourages him. With Theo's help he is introduced to the society of the new painters, the impressionists, and he is soon exposed to the theories of Pissarro, Toulouse-Lautrec,

With Anthony Quinn

Bernard, Seurat, and Paul Gauguin (Anthony Quinn), whom he particularly admires. He works hard at his painting but finds no buyers for his work. Van Gogh takes Gauguin's advice and heads for the south of France, to the lovely pastoral country of Provence. Living in Arles, Van Gogh's genius blossoms quickly and he soon becomes enormously productive.

Sensing that his brother must be protected from his own feverish energy, Theo persuades Gauguin to join Van Gogh in Arles. But both painters have definite, uncompromising theories about art, and about life, and their friendship soon dissipates. After Gau-

Painting "Stars at Night" with candles in his hat to give him light

Painting at the St. Remy institution

guin leaves, Van Gogh becomes depressive and in his anguish he mutilates an ear with a razor. Self-committed to a mental institution at St. Rémy, he makes a partial recovery but the intensity of his work brings on another violent fit. Van Gogh turns again to the man he knows will help. He proceeds to Paris to see his brother, who arranges for the distraught painter to be cared for by Dr. Gachet (Everett Sloane), a doctor sympathetic to the art world. Living in Auvers, Van Gogh tries to conserve his energies but he continues to paint, "like a miner who knows he is in danger," and he hopefully waits for the months to pass without an attack.

Toward the end of July, 1890, Vincent Van Gogh suffered the extreme mental depression that brought on his death. His last painting was a tortured, emotional canvas of a shimmering wheatfield, with a purple road cutting through the golden grain, as a

The last painting by Van Gogh—the wheatfield and the crows

Painting the drawbridge near Arles—the actual location of one of the most famous Van Gogh canvases

flight of black crows flutter overhead. For Van Gogh the crows were a harbinger of death. Shortly after finishing the canvas, he shot himself, dying a few hours later in the arms of his brother, unaware of his surpassing talent or that his works would endure and become acclaimed.

Lust for Life benefits enormously from the authenticity of its locations. The company filmed in Le Borinage, in Nuenen, The Hague, in Auvers-sur-Oise, and in their several weeks in Provence they filmed in the actual institution at St. Rémy where Van Gogh was hospitalized. In Arles they found two ancient citizens who had known Van Gogh when they were children, one of them being "The Baby Roulin" sixty-five years later. Perhaps the locations and the atmospheres inspired the cast and crew, because *Lust for Life* is an inspired film. Kirk Douglas was able to marshal his own brand of intensity to graphically suggest that of Van Gogh, a man possessed. It is a vivid, moving and pulsating piece of acting.

With Anthony Quinn

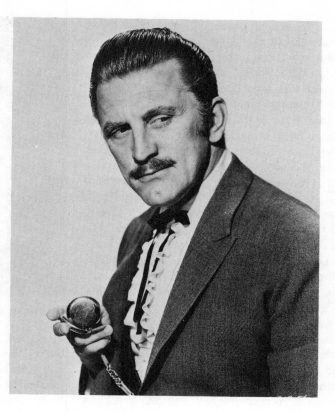

Gunfight at the O.K. Corral

1957   A Hal B. Wallis Production, *distributed by* Paramount. *Produced by* Hal B. Wallis. *Directed by* John Sturges. *Written by* Leon Uris. *Photographed in Technicolor by* Charles Lang, Jr. *Edited by* Warren Low. *Art directors,* Hal Pereira *and* Walter Tyler. *Musical score by* Dimitri Tiomkin. *Running time:* 122 minutes.

CAST: Burt Lancaster (*Wyatt Earp*), Kirk Douglas (*Doc Holliday*), Rhonda Fleming (*Laura Denbow*), Jo Van Fleet (*Kate Fisher*), John Ireland (*Ringo*), Lyle Bettger (*Ike Clanton*), Frank Faylen (*Cotton Wilson*), Earl Holliman (*Charles Bassett*), Ted De Corsia (*Shanghai Pierce*), Dennis Hopper (*Billy Clanton*), Whit Bissell (*John P. Clum*), George Mathews (*John Shanssey*), John Hudson (*Virgil Earp*), DeForrest Kelley (*Morgan Earp*), Martin Milner (*James Earp*), Kenneth Toby (*Bat Masterson*), Lee Van Cleef (*Ed Bailey*), Joan Camden (*Betty Earp*), Olive Carey (*Mrs. Clanton*), Brian Hutton (*Rick*), Nelson Leigh (*Mayor Kelley*), Jack Elam (*Tom McLowery*), Don Castle (*Drunken Cowboy*).

The question has yet to be solved: should the American West be depicted on the screen as it actually was, or should it continue to be a form of mythology? Hollywood's version of history is considerably at variance with the facts, and life on the frontier in the last century would appear to have been more dull and drab than exciting and colorful. Certainly, life in Tombstone, Arizona, in its heyday as a mining town must have been anything but healthy, with its hordes of rough working men relieving their boredom with drinking and brawling, and occasionally shooting each other. Its famed peace officer, lauded in so many novels and films—Wyatt Earp—is now said to have been a venal, law manipulating, brothel owner. His friend, Doc Holliday, is branded as an unsuccessful dentist with a particularly mean and murderous nature. Investigation proves the celebrated gunfight between Earp and Holliday and the Clanton gang to have been a fleeting matter, over in a few seconds, and not the drawnout battle of the legend. The setting, the subject and the characters have oft been used in movies, most distinctively by John Ford in *My Darling Clementine* (1946), with Henry Fonda as Earp and Victor Mature as Holliday. In his handsome 1957 version, *Gunfight at the O.K. Corral,* Hal B. Wallis cast his ex-alumni Burt Lancaster as Earp, and Kirk Douglas as Holliday, assigning John Sturges to direct, and the estimable Leon Uris to invent a screenplay. Wallis astutely brought in Charles Lang, Jr. to color photograph the proceedings and the landscapes, and Dimitri Tiomkin to back up the whole with a rousing symphonic score. The end result has little to do with history but it has a great deal to do with good entertainment.

The Uris screenplay concentrates on the friendship between Earp and Holliday, two different kinds of men and not, by logic, types who would be sympathetic to one another—Earp, the upright defender

With Burt Lancaster

of the law, and Holliday, a dissolute gambler. Nevertheless, the men are compassionate and respectful, and both have a kind of dignity. Holliday is the more interesting—the black sheep of an aristocratic Virginia family and a jaded idealist.

The story opens in Fort Griffin, Texas, as Earp, already famed as the tamer of Dodge City, saves

With Burt Lancaster

Holliday from a lynching. The scene then moves to Dodge City, where Holliday is not welcomed by the citizenry. Only Earp's intervention prevents Holliday from being driven from the town, although his stock increases rapidly when he helps Earp quell and capture three gunmen. Earp later receives a letter from his brother Virgil, who is the marshall of Tombstone, asking Wyatt for help in handling a gang who are terrorizing the town, the Clanton Brothers. Earp immediately packs his bags and heads west, accompanied by the fatalistic Holliday. The finale of the film is, inevitably, the showdown between the Earps, aided by Holliday, and the Clantons. After much shooting, justice prevails.

With Jo Van Fleet and John Ireland

With Burt Lancaster, John Hudson and DeForrest Kelly

With Burt Lancaster

Gunfight at the O.K. Corral is pure western fiction, magnificently served up. It is ample proof why film fables draw more customers than documentaries. With Wallis at the helm, his cast and his crew provide an exciting, rousing two hours of escapist fare. The dialogue and characterizations of Uris are sound and sure, and Sturges, a director with real feeling for outdoors action, times his movements as neatly as if he were conducting from a musical score. However, the two main assets of the film are Lancaster and Douglas, two stars thoroughly aware of their capabilities in this kind of material, and playing it to the hilt. Douglas tends to come off better, for the simple reason that the role of the quixotic, troubled Holliday is more dazzling stuff than the solid, self-assured style of Earp. Neurosis pays dividends—for actors at work. And Wild West nonsense is vastly enjoyable when concocted by experts.

With Burt Lancaster

Top Secret Affair

1957   A Warner Bros. Picture. *Produced by* Milton Sperling *and* Martin Rackin. *Directed by* H. C. Potter. *Written by* Roland Kibbee *and* Allan Scott, *based on characters from* Melville Goodwin, U.S.A. *by* John P. Marquand. *Photographed by* Stanley Cortez. *Edited by* Folmar Blangsted. *Art director,* Malcolm Bert. *Musical score by* Roy Webb. *Running time:* 100 minutes.

CAST: Susan Hayward *(Dottie Peale),* Kirk Douglas *(Maj. Gen. Melville Goodwin),* Paul Stewart *(Phil Bentley),* Jim Backus *(Col. Gooch),* John Cromwell *(Gen. Grimshaw),* Roland Winters *(Senator Burwick),* A. E. Gould-Porter *(Butler),* Michael Fox *(Lotzie),* Frank Gerstle *(Sgt. Kruger),* Charles Lane *(Bill Hadley).*

Warner Brothers purchased the rights to J. P. Marquand's novel *Melville Goodwin, USA,* with the idea of using it as a vehicle for Humphrey Bogart and Lauren Bacall. Bogart's illness changed the plans—ironically he died at the time the film was released (January, 1957)—and Kirk Douglas and Susan Hayward were assigned the lead roles. Warners also decided the plot of the Marquand novel was unsuitable for filming, and Roland Kibbee and Allan Scott were instructed to invent their own yarn, using only the Marquand characters. The resultant film is far from being a great comedy but it is an amusing farce-satire resting heavily on the fine performances of Douglas and Hayward. It manages to be funny on both sophisticated and slapstick levels, as well as being romantic—no mean trick in film making.

Hayward is a dynamic, powerful magazine publisher, somewhat suggestive of Clare Booth Luce and *Time,* and Douglas is a virile, fighting soldier with

With Susan Hayward

With Jim Backus

the rank of Major General. Hayward becomes irate when Douglas is given a government appointment, one she feels should have gone to the man she has been touting for the job. Out of spite, she decides to discredit the general. She invites him to her plush Long Island home, entertaining him as a guest but intent on studying him and trying to find things about

him and his career that might be used to his disadvantage. Before she is through, she discovers more about him than she bargained for—the general arouses more than her journalistic urges. Instead of exposing him, the fiery lady subsides in his arms. Inevitably, misunderstandings mar the course of love and Hayward reverts to her original plan when the general

With Susan Hayward

With Susan Hayward, Roland Winters and
Paul Stewart

With Susan Hayward

walks out on her. The exposé brings on a senatorial
investigation, in which her attempts to discredit him
backfire. The publisher has to admit she was wrong,
a concession that takes her back to the arms of the
virile warrior.

Top Secret Affair is full of bright lines and moments. The vivacious Hayward sparkles in both anger
and in passion, and the film gives Douglas the best
of his comedy roles. His general is publicity conscious
but he sees through the trap laid for him by the publisher. He proceeds to let her make a fool of him,
knowing that it is really the other way around. There
are some good comic interludes as Hayward takes
the general slumming, with photographers hidden
everywhere to catch him in compromising situations.
Especially funny is a scene at the publisher's home in
which she becomes increasingly tipsy, finally climbing
and balancing on a high diving board, as the sober
general calmly stands by, ready to fish her out of the
pool when she falls.

The film shoots barbs at the military, at Congress
and at the magazine publishing business. For the
most part the spoof is sharp without being rancorous.
As in all good film comedy, much of the effectiveness
lies in the expert casting of the supporting players.
Top Secret Affair boasts solid performances from
Paul Stewart as the publisher's cynical but genial

aide, Jim Backus as a perpetually confused Army
public relations officer, Roland Winters as a spiteful
senatorial investigator, and John Cromwell as a harried Army Chief of Staff. The shiny bits all fit into a
glossy package.

Paths of Glory

1957   A Harris-Kubrick Production, *distributed by* United Artists. *Produced by* James B. Harris. *Directed by* Stanley Kubrick. *Written by* Stanley Kubrick, Calder Willingham *and* Jim Thompson, *based on the novel by* Humphrey Cobb. *Photographed by* George Krause. *Edited by* Eva Kroll. *Art director,* Ludwig Reiber. *Musical score by* Gerald Fried. *Running time:* 86 minutes.

CAST: Kirk Douglas *(Colonel Dax),* Ralph Meeker *(Corporal Paris),* Adolphe Menjou *(General Broulard),* George Macready *(General Mireau),* Wayne Morris *(Lieutenant Roget),* Richard Anderson *(Major Saint-Auban),* Joseph Turkel *(Private Arnaud),* Timothy Carey *(Private Ferol),* Peter Capell *(Colonel Judge),* Susanne Christian *(German Girl),* Bert Freed *(Sergeant Boulanger),* Emile Meyer *(Priest),* John Stein *(Captain Rousseau).*

Paths of Glory is inevitably coupled with *All Quiet on the Western Front* as the two most heart rending and starkly realistic films about the lives of common soldiers in the trenches of the First World War. Ironically, although both films are American neither deals with American soldiers. Stanley Kubrick's *Paths of Glory* relates the miseries of French troops while Lewis Milestone's 1930 classic tells of futility and despair of German soldiers. Despite the similarity of subject matter the two films differ widely in their intent; the Milestone picture is clearly anti-war in feeling, its German soldiers speak up about the senselessness of their plight, whereas the Kubrick film deals with the business of fighting in the trenches and of injustice within the French Army. The No-Man's-Land in *Paths of Glory* is more the gulf between officers and men than the gap between enemy armies. Purportedly based on a true incident, the film has never been shown in France, such is the harrowing light it sheds upon French military politics in "the war to end all wars."

The story begins in September of 1916. The

With George Macready

weary 701st Infantry Regiment, decimated by months of futile battle, is due for rest. They are commanded by Colonel Dax, a peacetime criminal lawyer and a compassionate officer. Behind the front lines, at a picturesque chateau serving as headquarters, General Mireau (George Macready), the division commander, receives General Broulard (Adolphe Menjou), the corps commander representing the General Staff. He comes to tell Mireau that his division must take the Ant Hill, an impregnable German fortification, within the next forty-eight hours. Mireau voices his opinion that the mission is impossible but he is persuaded by the implication of promotion. Mireau visits the trenches and gives Dax his orders; Dax angrily protests but Mireau threatens to relieve him of his command, whereupon he accepts the orders, feeling that he cannot desert the men who know and respect him. At nightfall Dax sends a reconnaissance patrol to scout

the area leading to the Ant Hill. The attack starts the next morning, accompanied by thunderous volleys of artillery. The Frenchmen make very little progress across the pitted, scarred, muddy wasteland leading to the German lines. When platoons of the French regiment are unable to leave their trenches due to the intensity of the German shelling, General Mireau furiously orders his own artillery to fire upon the cowering French infantrymen. The artillery commander refuses unless the general puts the order in writing. The French attack on the Ant Hill is an abysmal failure, impractical in its concept and utterly impossible in its execution.

Mireau orders the regiment withdrawn and placed under collective arrest. He demands that one section of each company be tried under penalty of death for mutiny and cowardice. Dax realizes the general is looking for a scapegoat to cover his and the general staff's fantastic error in judgment. He argues with Mireau and Broulard and eventually the generals settle for the execution of just three men, one from each company. Dax receives only one concession, that he be allowed to act as defense counsel for his men. The trial is held in the Grand Ballroom of the chateau but it is a travesty of justice. It is soon apparent that no defense is possible and that the verdict is obvious—the men must die. Declares Dax, "There are times when I am ashamed to be a member of the human race. This is one such occasion."

A ray of hope dawns with the revelation to Dax by the artillery captain that he was ordered by Mireau to fire on his own men. Dax proceeds to the chateau

to confer with Broulard; arriving during the lavish dinner party, Dax gets Broulard's attention but not the reaction he had anticipated. Broulard will not sacrifice General Mireau and he dismisses Dax. The executions must take place as specified. Meanwhile, the three doomed soldiers spend their last hours in a dank cellar, vainly comforted by a priest. One of the

With George Macready and Richard Anderson

With Wayne Morris (right)

soldiers loses his mind and attacks the priest, but he is knocked down by one of the others and his skull is fractured. At the time of execution the injured soldier is carried unconscious on a stretcher to his stake. Paraded in front of the chateau, the regiment watch while the three men are shot to death by a firing squad.

After the execution General Broulard calls in Mireau and Dax to announce that Mireau will face a court of inquiry for ordering his artillery to fire on his own men. When the outraged Mireau leaves, Broulard offers his post to Dax. Sickened by the offer, Dax refuses and retires. On his way back to his quarters Dax stops outside a café, made curious by the sounds inside. He finds his soldiers hooting at a captured German girl trying to entertain them with a song. Dax is disgusted that his men should so quickly have forgotten their comrades, but the Ger-

With Adolphe Menjou

ing barns, destroying the vegetation and shredding the trees with explosives. Sixty workmen labored for three weeks digging crater holes, strewing barbed wire, littring the fields with debris and churning them into muddy ruts and gullies. The area was then wired with hundreds of explosives, operated by a staff of electricians. In the interest of dramatic effect, Kubrick made one compromise with realism in filming his trench sequences. He had his trenches dug six feet wide in order to make room for his rolling camera. Kubrick was thus able to achieve the long, continuous tracking shots through the trenches—shots that are visually remarkable and allow for quick and harrowing trips through the ghastly men-encrusted ruts.

Colonel Dax is one of Kirk Douglas' most effective performances but in discussing the picture he feels the performance is merely part of the fabric of the picture and that *Paths of Glory* should be viewed as a whole, as an entity. The credit belongs, says Douglas, to Kubrick. Be that as it may, *Paths of Glory* is marked by distinguished acting, by the tough compassionate colonel of Douglas and especially by Adolphe Menjou as the foxy Broulard and by George Macready as the cold-blooded patrician Mireau. It is a masterly, disturbing and haunting film.

man girl is so touching and poignant in her simple singing that the Frenchmen are soon humming along with her. The anger leaves Dax's face and fades into understanding. As a sergeant approaches to announce that the troops have been ordered back to the front, Dax tells him to give the men a few moments more of relaxation. He then slowly turns and walks back to his quarters.

Paths of Glory is an almost faultless picture. Its script, its direction, its acting and its settings blend into a perfect story telling form. The scenes in the depressing trenches contrast sharply with those in the great baroque chateau. The callousness of the French officers in deploying their troops against the enemy and speaking of calculated percentage losses is more frightening than the enemy himself. The trial, conducted in a huge chamber of the chateau, its floor composed of black and white squares, is conducted like a hideous chess game. The scenes of warfare are fluidly directed by Kubrick to appear almost like actual film footage of the First World War.

The film was shot in Germany and the battlefield was built near the village of Pucheim, twenty-five miles west of Munich. The company rented the ground and then turned it into a quagmire of war, demolish-

The Vikings

1958 A Bryna Production, *distributed by* United Artists. *Produced by* Jerry Bresler. *Directed by* Richard Fleischer. *Written by* Calder Willingham, *adapted by* Dale Wasserman *from the novel The Viking by* Edison Marshall. *Photographed in Technicolor by* Jack Cardiff. *Edited by* Elmo Williams. *Produc-tion designer,* Harper Goff. *Musical score by* Mario Nascimbene. *Running time:* 114 minutes.

CAST: Kirk Douglas *(Einar),* Tony Curtis *(Eric),* Ernest Borgnine *(Ragnar),* Janet Leigh

With James Donald and Ernest Borgnine   With James Donald

(Morgana), James Donald *(Egbert)*, Alexander Knox *(Father Godwin)*, Frank Thring *(Aella)*, Maxine Audley *(Enid)*, Eileen Way *(Kitala)*, Edric Connor *(Sandpiper)*, Dandy Nichols *(Bridget)*, Per Buchhij *(Bjorn)*, Almut Berg *(Pigtails)*.

Most reviewers have been facetious in dealing with *The Vikings,* referring to is as a "Norse Opera" and commenting that the great expense and effort spent on the historically accurate sets and costumes is at variance with its probable audience, i.e., the juvenile trade, and admirers of gore and violence on the screen. Provided he is willing to tolerate the banality of the story, the history student will find much to catch his eye, beginning with the film's credit titles. These were designed by the UPA studio, and give animation to figures suggested by the Bayeux tapestry, setting up the historical background of the story. The interiors of the film were shot in the Geiselgasteig Studios in Munich, and the exteriors were shot in Norway and on the coast of Brittany. Most interestingly, the company built replicas of the Viking vessels on display in Oslo's Viking Museum. These ships range in length from sixty-five to seventy-five feet, and require huge teams of oarsmen. To row their replicas, the company hired a couple of hundred members of rowing clubs in Norway and Denmark. The sequence showing the invasion of England was actually filmed in France, at Fort La Lotte, because it was in better shape than its tenth century counter-

parts across the Channel. All this visual grandeur was magnificently color photographed by Jack Cardiff, soon to become a director himself. Some of his shots, especially scenes of the Viking ships in fjords, are mystically beautiful.

The Vikings attempts to document the period in Norse history when the Vikings, worshippers of Odin, the pagan God of War, tried to conquer England, which at that time was a series of small, divided kingdoms. The film plays against this background a narrative of lust and bloodletting, love and hate, as Eric (Tony Curtis), symbolizing the traditional hero of mythology, emerges from obscurity and performs the deeds of daring, predestined to win him warrior status and his place as leader of his people. The opening scenes present a vivid introduction to Norse savagery as Ragnar (Ernest Borgnine), a Viking king, invades the English coast and pillages everything in his path. He kills the English King and rapes the Queen, who later has to confess to her loyal friend Father Godwin (Alexander Knox) that she is pregnant. Some years later, King Aella (Frank Thring), the successor, announces that in order to strengthen their defenses against the Vikings, he will unite the kingdoms of Northumbria and Wales by marrying the Welsh princess Morgana (Janet Leigh), a price the lovely young lady is not eager to pay. The mean King also turns upon his upright cousin Lord Egbert (James Donald) and accuses him of espionage, and has him thrown into jail. Egbert is rescued from certain death by Ragnar, in a return visit, and the grateful man throws in his lot with the Norsemen,

Back in Norway, Ragnar is greeted by his son Einar (Kirk Douglas) who is instantly hostile to the Englishman. While showing Egbert some Viking customs, Einar comes across a pair of slaves, one of whom is Eric. Apparently captured as a child, he has grown up among the Vikings. He and Einar, half-brothers but unaware of the fact, become enemies when Eric insults the Norse chieftain, and they fight, during which Einar loses one of his eyes. Eric stands trial and is punished by being cast into a slop-pool to be eaten alive by giant crabs. Egbert notices a royal pummel-stone Eric wears around his neck, and aware that the Queen mother had placed such an ornament on her illegitimate offspring, he suspects the identity of Eric and arranges with Ragnar for his rescue. When Morgana is captured, as arranged by Ragnar and Egbert, and brought to Norway, she and Eric fall in love, to the consternation of Einar, who would like to have the princess for himself.

Eric and Morgana escape and make their way back to England. Einar and Ragnar pursue but lose their way in the fog and crash on the rocks in the fjord—Eric saves Ragnar from drowning and takes him back to England to use as a pawn to win a favor from King Aella, still enraged over the loss of Morgana. In exchange for Ragnar, Eric hopes to win the hand of the princess. When Ragnar is thrown into a wolf-pit to die, Eric gives him his sword so that he may die like a warrior, for which act the King orders Eric thrown in, too. He is saved by the pleading of Morgana, but he has to pay with the loss of his left

With Janet Leigh

hand and in being cast adrift in the North Sea. Eric somehow manages to find his way back to Norway and when he explains to Einar what has happened, the two men decide to set aside their hatred for each other and unite in an attack against the kingdom of Aella.

With Tony Curtis

With Janet Leigh

The final scenes of *The Vikings* are devoted to the invasion and the bloody hand-to-hand fighting as the Vikings vanquish the Englishmen. Einar reaches Morgana first and proclaims his love for her, but she again rejects him. When he says he will kill Eric, she reveals her knowledge of the two men being half-brothers. When Eric appears on the scene, the two engage in a savage sword fight but at the moment when Einar is about to plunge his weapon into the younger man, he hesitates, obviously halted by the knowledge he may be killing a brother. Eric, unaware that Einar knows, seizes the opportunity and stabs Einar. In the film's last scene, Einar receives the tra-ditional Viking funeral, his ship sailing to Valhalla in flames.

The Vikings, a lavish and expensive vehicle, is one of Kirk Douglas' own productions and one of which he is especially fond. When asked for his favorites among his own films, he always includes a mention of *The Vikings*. It is, captiousness aside, a handsome piece of entertainment, splendidly mounted, and it serves as an illustration of the lifestyle of the ferocious Norse warriors whose idea of fun-and-games was almost as lethal as their warfare. If this picture is to be believed, we have every reason to be glad a thousand years removes us from their company.

With Tony Curtis, Ernest Borgnine and James Donald

With Tony Curtis

With Ziva Rodann

Last Train from Gun Hill

1959   A Hal B. Wallis Production, *distributed by* Paramount. *Produced by* Hal B. Wallis. *Directed by* John Sturges. *Written by* James Poe, *based on a story by* Les Crutchfield. *Photographed by Technicolor by* Charles Lang, Jr. *Edited by* Warren Low. *Art Directors,* Hal Pereira *and* Walter Tyler. *Musical score by* Dimitri Tiomkin. *Running time:* 94 minutes.

CAST: Kirk Douglas *(Matt Morgan),* Anthony Quinn *(Craig Belden),* Carolyn Jones *(Linda),* Earl Holliman *(Rick Belden),* Brad Dexter *(Beero),* Brian Hutton *(Lee),* Ziva Rodann *(Catherine Morgan),* Bing Russell *(Skag),* Val Avery *(Bartender),* Walter Sande *(Sheriff Bartlett),* Lars Henderson *(Petey Morgan).*

With the great success of *Gunfight at the O.K. Corral,* Hal B. Wallis called on Kirk Douglas to do another western for him, giving him the same director, John Sturges, and some of the same crew—cinematographer Charles Lang, Jr., composer Dimitri Tiomkin, art directors Hal Pereira and Walter Tyler, and editor Warren Low. With a script by James Poe, *Last Train from Gun Hill* is in the same league of quality with Douglas' previous Wallis western but it is a story on a smaller scale, and in some ways more plausible. While it may lack some of the popular appeal of

Gunfight, this is a slightly more adult story and the characters and the dialogue are more believable. Again it is largely a stylistic battle between two superb film actors—here it is Anthony Quinn instead of Burt Lancaster—and again, the direction, the photography, the scoring, the art work and the editing are of the highest calibre.

Sturges sets up his atmosphere of dramatic tension right at the start: two young range roughs, Rick Belden (Earl Holliman) and Lee (Brian Hutton) spot a beautiful squaw (Ziva Rodann), with her son Petey (Lars Henderson), as they are out riding in the country. They molest, rape, and then kill the woman, while the boy escapes by jumping on the horse of one of the assailants and riding off. The boy is the son of Matt Morgan (Kirk Douglas), the marshal of the small town of Pauley, Oklahoma. The widower lawman sets out to find his wife's murderers. His main

With Anthony Quinn

With Carolyn Jones

clue is the expensive saddle on the horse taken by his son. He recognizes the saddle as belonging to an old friend, Craig Belden, a cattle baron and the most powerful man in the neighboring town of Gun Hill. Morgan visits Belden, who once saved his life, and the two men greet each other warmly and with genuine respect. Belden expresses his disgust over the repulsive crime, but a little investigation reveals that the culprit is his own spineless son, Rick, aided by Lee, who is also in Belden's employ. Belden throws Lee off the ranch but he cannot bring himself to turn in his son.

A man now torn between justice and familial loyalty, Belden elects to prevent Morgan from carrying out his mission. He organizes the townspeople to save his son, even though he is revolted by the character of the boy. Eventually, Morgan gains entrance to the saloon in which Rick is secreted, and after

station platform for the inevitable settling of accounts. In the fast-draw contest, Belden is the loser, and Morgan gets on the train and leaves Gun Hill.

The expertise before the cameras and behind it makes *Last Train from Gun Hill* a respectable entry in the annals of the best westerns. Douglas and Quinn carry the burden of the drama but they get fine help from Carolyn Jones as the mistress and Earl Holliman as the weak son of a strong father. The film is taught and tight, and the suspense never flags, all of which is a credit to John Sturges.

With Earl Holliman

With Anthony Quinn

knocking him unconscious, Morgan throws Rick over his shoulder and makes his way to a hotel, there to wait for the next train out of Gun Hill, the last one of the day. Belden and his men lay siege to the hotel and it seems there is little hope of Morgan being able to make his train. But he picks up an unexpected ally in Linda (Carolyn Jones), the caustic mistress of Belden. Willing as she is to forgive the beatings of Belden, her loathing for his weakling son is so strong she feels compelled to see him get his fit punishment. Linda gives Morgan a shotgun; this he sticks under the chin of Rick as the two of them walk from the hotel to the railroad station. The hot-headed Lee now tries to come to the aid of his friend, but he inadvertently kills him and is himself shot down by Morgan. With Rick dead, Belden faces Morgan on the

The Devil's Disciple

1959   A co-production of Hecht-Hill-Lancaster Films, *and* Brynaprod, S.A., *distributed by* United Artists. *Produced by* Harold Hecht. *Directed by* Guy Hamilton. *Written by* John Dighton *and* Roland Kibbee, *based on the play by* George Bernard Shaw. *Photographed by* Jack Hildyard. *Edited by* Alan Osbiston. *Art Directors,* Terrence Verity *and* Edward Carrere. *Musical score by* Richard Rodney Bennett. *Running time:* 82 minutes.

CAST: Burt Lancaster (*Anthony Anderson*), Kirk Douglas (*Richard Dudgeon*), Laurence Olivier (*General Burgoyne*), Janette Scott (*Judith Anderson*), Eva LeGallienne (*Mrs. Dudgeon*), Harry Andrews (*Major Swindon*), Basil Sydney (*Lawyer Hawkins*), George Rose (*British Sergeant*), Neil McCallum (*Christopher Dudgeon*), Mervyn Johns (*Rev. Maindeck Parshotter*), David Horne (*William*).

Kirk Douglas and Burt Lancaster not only co-starred in *The Devil's Disciple,* they were responsible for the film being made. Douglas' company, Brynaprod, joined forces with Hecht-Hill-Lancaster to produce this rather odd choice of vehicle. *The Devil's Disciple* has never been regarded as one of the better works of George Bernard Shaw; Shaw himself was dissatisfied with the play when it was read at the copyright performance in London in 1897 and refused to let it be staged in England. The play was first staged in the United States with the celebrated Richard Mansfield

With Burt Lancaster

With Janette Scott

playing Richard Dudgeon—played by Douglas in the film—and with its American success Shaw relented and allowed British versions. The screenplay by John Dighton hews closely to the original although it allows more accenting of the roles played by its American stars, both of whom were wise enough as producers to hire Laurence Olivier to play the plum role of Major General John Burgoyne. Without Olivier and his subtle playing of the suave, witty

soldier, this version of *The Devil's Disciple* would sag disastrously. The film was not a major success but it nonetheless provides much amusement, although Shavian purists had reason to fear the worst when they saw newspaper ads for the picture, such as "Burt, Kirk and Larry are coming—by George!"

The setting of *The Devil's Disciple* is New England at the time of the War for Independence. Shaw takes as his focal point the fatuous blunders of the

With George Rose and Janette Scott

British Army in their campaigns against the American colonists. The Irish playwright ever enjoyed needling the English Establishment, and at the end of this play Shaw had his philosophical Burgoyne comfort his second-in-command, concerned over the defeat of his soldiers by the Americans: "Take it quietly, Swindon. Your friend, the British soldier can stand up to anything—except the British War Office." In point of fact, it was the conflicting orders and lack of communication with London that defeated the British military efforts in America. Shaw used this sentiment to color his story, hence the sympathy is almost entirely with the Americans, not that they escaped unscathed—greed and opportunism of any stripe caught Shaw's eye and tongue.

The Devil's Disciple takes place in a small town, taken over by Burgoyne and his men when they march down from Canada. To subdue the rebellious colonists, the British hang a prominent citizen, Timothy Dudgeon. The village pastor, Anthony Anderson (Lancaster), arrives home to find his young wife (Janette Scott) comforting the widow. Soon after, the

With George Rose, Laurence Olivier and Janette Scott

With Burt Lancaster

hanged man's rakehell son Richard (Douglas) descends on the community to cause trouble for the British garrison and chide any colonials who won't support the revolution. The dashing, roguish Dick Dudgeon causes ripples in the Anderson household; the quiet pastor secretly admires Dudgeon's attitude but he becomes concerned when his pretty young wife begins to evince admiration of her own. The jaunty Burgoyne, who would much rather be socializing in London than commanding a distasteful campaign, allows himself to be talked into hanging another rebel as an example. They pick on the pastor. When the soldiers arrive at the Anderson home, they find Dudgeon, and assume him to be the pastor. Partly as a whim and partly to help the pastor, who has fled and joined the revolutionary forces, Dudgeon allows himself to be arrested and tried. The pastor's wife now finds her feelings for the gallant Dudgeon blossoming into love.

Pastor Anderson turns into a tiger of a soldier. He intercepts an important message destined for Burgoyne, and he uses the message as an ace-in-the-hole when he faces Burgoyne and dickers for the life of Dudgeon, who is then saved from hanging an instant before the noose is put around his neck. Now a hero

to his wife, the pastor regains her love—while Dudgeon accepts an invitation to join the General for afternoon tea. A commentator ends the picture by telling us that Burgoyne surrendered at Saratoga only three weeks later.

Douglas and Lancaster are excellent as the rake who becomes idealistic and the minister who turns fighter. Their lines and characters keep them somewhat hemmed in, but Douglas is suitably cavalier as Dudgeon, and Lancaster comes vividly alive in a scene where he knocks the stuffing out of a group of British soldiers, beating them with solemn, religious thoroughness. The scene is amusing and Lancaster is well in form. But the lion's share of humor in *The Devil's Disciple* is meted out by Olivier as the urbane Burgoyne, a genuinely interesting historical character whose manners and stylish behavior earned him the sobriquet "Gentleman Johnny." Olivier effortlessly tosses off Shavian quips, such as, "Martyrdom, sir, is the only way in which a man can become famous without ability." In perhaps the best line in the film, he explains to Dudgeon, who asks to be shot rather than hanged, that hanging would be less painful, "Have you any idea of the average marksmanship of the Army of His Majesty, King George III?"

Strangers When We Meet

1960   A Bryna-Quine Production, *distributed by Columbia Pictures. Produced and directed by* Richard Quine. *Written by* Evan Hunter, *based on his novel. Photographed in CinemaScope and Eastmancolor by* Charles Lang, Jr. *Edited by* Charles Nelson. *Art director,* Ross Bellah. *Musical score by* George Duning. *Running time:* 117 minutes.

CAST: Kirk Douglas (*Larry Coe*), Kim Novak (*Maggie Gault*), Ernie Kovacs (*Roger Altar*), Barbara Rush (*Eve Coe*), Walter Matthau (*Felix Anders*), Virginia Bruce (*Mrs. Wagner*), Kent Smith (*Stanley Baxter*), Helen Gallagher (*Betty Anders*), John Bryant (*Ken Gault*), Roberta Shore (*Linda Harder*), Nancy Kovak (*Marcia*), Carol Douglas (*Honey Blonde*), Paul Picerni (*Gerandi*), Ernest Sarracino (*Di Labbia*), Harry Jackson (*Bud Ramsey*), Bart Patton (*Hank*), Robert Sampson (*Bucky*), Ray Ferrell (*David Coe*), Douglas Holmes (*Peter Coe*), Timmy Molina (*Patrick Gault*).

At the time of its release in 1960, *Strangers When We Meet* was considered to be daring in its frankness about adultery and sexual straying among upper-middle-class American suburbanites. By the end of

With Kim Novak

expertise. *Strangers When We Meet* truly has more production values than it deserves; the color photography of the more plush parts of Los Angeles and the nearby beaches by Charles Lang, Jr., and the stunning work of art director Ross Bellah should belong to a weightier vehicle.

Kirk Douglas here appears as a brilliant and idealistic architect named Larry Coe. He has a lovely wife, Eve (Barbara Rush), and two young sons, but he falls in love with a beautiful, married neighbor, Margaret (Kim Novak), who also has a son but is unhappy with her husband, Ken (John Bryant). Larry is commissioned by a writer, Roger Altar (Ernie Kovacs), to build a mountain-top home for him. Aside from his writing, Altar is noted for his love of young ladies, the variety of whom do not solve his basic loneliness.

As Larry progresses with the Altar house, so he progresses with his illicit affair with Margaret, meeting mainly at a cocktail lounge on the coast. Inevitably, his wife hears about the affair and she questions him, to little avail. The lovers agree to part but they are soon drawn together again. Eve gives a party for the neighbors, including Margaret and her husband, and Felix Anders (Walter Matthau) and his wife (Helen Gallagher), a far from happy couple. Felix

the '60's, with the cinema swamped with commercial candor, the film appeared fairly tepid. But even at the time of issue, it was still basically a slight story, of the kind usually found in pulp magazines of love confessions, and given copious gloss with Hollywood

With Barbara Rush

With Kim Novak

With Ernie Kovacs

considers all women fair game. He kids Larry about the range of opportunities an architect must have for "playing around" and it becomes obvious he knows of the affair.

The emotionally distraught architect is next offered a great opportunity—to build a city in Hawaii. He holds back from telling his wife of the offer but goes to Margaret and suggests that they break with their families and start a new life together. To his considerable surprise, Larry finds her unwilling to leave her husband and son, telling him she would prefer things to stay as they are. At about the same time, the wily Felix visits the Coe home and makes a play for Eve. She repulses him and Felix leaves the house just as Larry is about to arrive. When Larry learns from his wife what has just happened, he runs after Felix and knocks him down with a punch in the face. But Felix gives him food for thought as he looks up and asks, "Tell me how I'm any different from you?" Larry and Eve are now forced to squarely face the issue—to stay together or part. She pleads with him to continue the marriage. Later Larry meets with Margaret at their rendezvous on the coast and

With Walter Matthau

he explains his decision, to keep his family and to accept the Hawaii commission. Margaret understands.

In less expert hands, *Strangers When We Meet* would be little more than just another trite tale of infidelity, but Douglas and Kim Novak play their parts with conviction. They are aided by the fine playing of Barbara Rush as the offended wife, Ernie Kovacs as the amusingly eccentric writer, and Walter Matthau as the queasy opportunist. It is all soap-opera but it glitters under the skillful guidance of producer-director Richard Quine. Mr. Quine was, at the time, apparently enamored of the lovely Miss Novak. He also inherited the fabulous house built for the picture, the one Douglas is seen designing for Kovacs. These factors possibly account for some of the shine on *Strangers When We Meet*.

With Kim Novak

Spartacus

1960   A Bryna Production for Universal-International. *Executive producer,* Kirk Douglas. *Produced by* Edward Lewis. *Directed by* Stanley Kubrick. *Written by* Dalton Trumbo, *based on the novel by* Howard Fast. *Photographed in Technicolor* by Russell Metty, *with additional photography by* Clifford Stine. *Edited by* Robert Lawrence. *Art director,* Eric Orbom. *Musical score by* Alex North. *Running time:* 190 minutes.

CAST: Kirk Douglas *(Spartacus),* Laurence Olivier *(Crassus),* Jean Simmons *(Varinia),* Tony Curtis *(Antoninus),* Charles Laughton *(Gracchus),* Peter Ustinov *(Batiatus),* John Gavin *(Julius Caesar),* Nina Foch *(Helena),* Herbert Lom *(Tigranes),* John Ireland *(Crixus),* John Dall *(Glabrus),* Charles McGraw *(Marcellus),* Joanna Barnes *(Claudia),* Harold J. Stone *(David),* Woody Strode *(Draba),* Peter Brocco *(Ramon),* Paul Lambert *(Gannicus),*

Douglas, second captive from the right. Peter Ustinov with back to camera. Charles McGraw at right

[167]

With Jean Simmons

Nicholas Dennis *(Dionysius),* Robert J. Wilke *(Guard Captain),* John Hoyt *(Roman Officer),* Frederic Worlock *(Laelius),* Dayton Lummis *(Symmachus).*

Kirk Douglas has reason to be proud of *Spartacus.* Of all the massive road-show movies dealing with ancient history it is by far the most intelligently written and directed, and it laced its lavish canvas with some moral and spiritual fibers. As the film's executive producer, and driving force, Douglas raised and spent twelve million dollars and involved himself for more than a year in production, including 167 days of actual filming. The result was a film of genuine merit, and quite apart from the believability of his performance as the Thracian slave who leads a revolt against Rome in the century before Christ, Douglas rates credit for the courage of hiring the then thirty-two-year-old Stanley Kubrick to direct the huge picture, and for engaging Dalton Trumbo to write it. Trumbo in 1960 was still *persona non grata* because of his political blacklisting and *Spartacus* was his first screen credit since his fall from grace in 1947, although he had written scripts in the meantime under pseudonyms. The book on which the film was based was written by Howard Fast, an admitted ex-Communist, but despite the political implications, what emerged on the screen was a passionate statement on behalf of freedom and men who are willing to die to overthrow oppressive governments.

The script of *Spartacus* hews fairly closely to history although the exact circumstances of his origin and death are obscure. He was, however, killed in battle and not crucified as depicted in the film. Spartacus was the leader of a band of seventy-eight slaves who escaped from the gladiatorial school at Capua, 130 miles south of Rome, in the year 73 B.C. He and his followers eluded the Roman armies, stole weapons and pillaged estates, and gradually built up a fighting force. After two years of revolt, Spartacus headed an

John Ireland behind Douglas. Charles McGraw with his arm on the training model

army of ninety thousand men, and they won every encounter with Roman legions. His men, emboldened by victory, persuaded him to tackle the main body of the Roman Army. They were decisively beaten and Spartacus was hacked to pieces on the battlefield. Six thousand of his men were later crucified along the Appian Way. Ever after, Spartacus has been an idealized figure to revolutionaries. The film made from these facts clearly upholds the spirit of the story, if not the actual facts. Not unexpectedly, certain politically conservative critics trounced *Spartacus,* but an impartial viewing of the film finds little sentiment differing from the tenor of the American Bill of Rights.

Spartacus is no mean epic. It is a pictorial crammed with detail, and its violence and crudity are thoroughly valid. The credit for the film's style belongs to Stanley Kubrick, who handled scenes of intimacy and scenes of gigantic sweep with equal attention. None of the performers got lost, as often happens in films of this kind. Kubrick later complained that he was not given sufficient freedom over script and content but this would appear to be somewhat ungrateful; he had not directed a film since *Paths of Glory* three years previously, despite critical acclaim, and *Spartacus* provided him with a considerable stepping stone to the success he afterwards enjoyed.

With Jean Simmons, Nina Foch, Laurence Olivier, John Dall, Joanna Barnes, and Woody Strode with his back to camera

Filming fight with Woody Strode

With director Stanley Kubrick

Douglas on a day off, visiting Peter Ustinov, Joanna Barnes, Nina Foch and Laurence Olivier

A number of critics snidely pointed to Kirk Douglas being outclassed by his fellow actors Laurence Olivier, Peter Ustinov, and Charles Laughton. This is a moot point. The brilliance and subtlety of the British actors is undeniable yet it is questionable if any one of them could have played the title role with the kind of muscular, brutish intensity that Douglas brought to the part. As with certain other roles that

The revolt of the student gladiators: John Ireland behind Douglas

With Laurence Olivier

who spots Spartacus working as a road gang laborer and buys him to train as a gladiator. The fleshy Laughton squirmed with expertise as Gracchus, an unctuous Roman politician, and Olivier played Crassus, a powerful patrician and a sly epicene degenerate. A scene in which Crassus attempts to seduce his handsome servant Antoninus (Tony Curtis) was cut from the film, thereby diminishing the resolve of Antoninus to escape Rome and join *Spartacus*. The producers considered this offensive to 1960 audiences; also several incidents of bloodletting were deleted. Such cuts would not have been made a decade later—whether this is a matter of maturity or of exploitation is open to endless debate.

The first half hour of *Spartacus* contains many of the film's best moments. The operation of the gladiatorial school and its training program is impressive and expressive; the apprentice gladiators are treated like special animals, tutored to perform in the arena as spectator-sport-killers, and occasionally rewarded with a woman in their cells. In this degrading manner Spartacus meets Varinia (Jean Simmons) and it is his love for her and his hatred for his captors that brings about his resolve to escape and lead revolt. Particularly effective is the scene in which Olivier and his bored entourage visit the school and ask for an exhibition. Spartacus is matched with Draba (Woody Strode) in a fight to the death, but Draba cannot bring

have captured his imagination, Douglas was totally committed to playing *Spartacus*. The fierceness of these committed roles makes him an unusual actor.

The performances of Olivier, Ustinov, and Laughton are, of course, superlative. Ustinov won an Oscar for playing Batiatus, a venal, conniving slave dealer

With Jean Simmons

himself to kill Spartacus and attacks his spectators, dying in the attempt. The scene summarizes the iniquity of the situation, the cruelty of bondage, and the subsequent escape of the gladiators from the school becomes a triumph easy to understand.

Spartacus contains no chariot races and no orgies but it still conveys the grandeur and the decay of ancient Rome. It does contain one of the most impressive battles yet staged for films: while much of the picture was shot on the Universal lot in Hollywood, Douglas took his large company to Spain for the exteriors and he employed eight thousand Spanish soldiers for the battle in which the Romans devastate the rebel army. The battle is filmed spaciously and clearly and the awesome vistas—in 70 mm. Technirama—give a sense of the horror and futility of massed hand-to-hand combat. *Spartacus* cannot be faulted in its technical excellence, in its staging and costuming, and in its musical scoring by Alex North, a text book example of the skillful use of music in films.

Tony Curtis, left of Douglas, and Harold J. Stone to the right

With Dorothy Malone

The Last Sunset

1961   A Brynaprod, S.A. Production for Universal-International. *Produced by* Eugene Frenke *and* Edward Lewis. *Directed by* Robert Aldrich. *Written by* Dalton Trumbo, *based on the novel Sundown at Crazy Horse by* Howard Rigsby. *Photographed by Eastmancolor by* Ernest Laszlo. *Edited by* Edward Mann. *Art directors,* Alexander Golitzen *and* Al Sweeney. *Musical score by* Ernest Gold. *Running time:* 112 minutes.

CAST: Rock Hudson *(Dana Stribling)*, Kirk Douglas *(Brendan O'Malley)*, Dorothy Malone *(Belle Breckenridge)*, Joseph Cotten *(John Breckenridge)*, Carol Lynley *(Missy Breckenridge)*, Neville Brand *(Frank Hobbs)*, Regis Toomey *(Milton Wing)*, Rad Fulton *(Julesberg Kid)*, Adam Williams *(Bowman)*, Jack Elam *(Ed Hobbs)*, John Shay *(Calverton)*, Margarito De Luna *(Jose)*, Jose Torvay *(Rosario)*.

The western has frequently been discussed as a form of Greek tragedy—its plotlines being simplistic and its human motivations basic. *The Last Sunset* fits this reasoning, telling as it does the story of a lonely, spiritually troubled drifter called Brendan O'Malley (Kirk Douglas), who dresses in black and poetically philosophizes about life. The film also brings in, possibly for the first time in a western, the suggestion of incest, with the resultant guilt leading to what is virtually a suicide. The script by Dalton Trumbo is not one in which he has expressed any great pride, and the long film was rather turgidly directed by Robert Aldrich, but *The Last Sunset* does contain a number of fine moments and interesting insights into western life.

The film opens with O'Malley being pursued into Mexico by a lawman from Texas, Dana Stribling (Rock Hudson). O'Malley is guilty of murder but he is unaware that the man he killed was the brother-in-law of the lawman. He takes it into his head to visit an old sweetheart, Belle Breckenridge (Dorothy Malone), whom he hasn't seen for sixteen years, and he

With Rock Hudson

finds her to have a sixteen-year-old daughter, Missy (Carol Lynley). Her husband is a drunken, garrulous southern gentleman-rancher, John (Joseph Cotten), who needs men to facilitate the driving of his cattle herd to Texas. O'Malley accepts the offer of employment but his terms are high—a fifth of the herd, plus Mrs. Breckenridge. John agrees to the first term but laughs off the second. When Stribling arrives on the scene, O'Malley talks him into joining the group as trail-boss, at which he is experienced. The glib O'Malley reasons that since the lawman has to turn him in at the very town to which the cattle drive is headed, they might as well work along the way.

The trip sees many developments: John Breckenridge is killed in a barroom brawl, but O'Malley finds his widow uninterested in taking up their former

With Joseph Cotton and Rock Hudson

With Rock Hudson

association. Instead, it is Stribling who falls in love with Belle, and she with him, while the lovely young Missy takes a shine to O'Malley that eventually turns to love. The two men, although enemies, come to respect each other. Three bushwackers join the group as trail drivers although their intention is to abduct the two women for the price they will bring on the white slave market. They fail in this ambition, paying with their lives. When Indians attack, the impetuous O'Malley shoots one and drives off the others. Knowing that a full scale attack would soon wipe them out, Stribling tries another approach. He picks up the corpse and returns it to the tribe, returning some while later with the Indians who then cut out a section of the herd and quietly drift away. Stribling tersely tells O'Malley he has just lost his fifth.

With Regis Toomey and Carol Lynley

The cattle drive is completed successfully and O'Malley and Stribling realize they must now come to terms, although the lawman no longer has the sense of vengeance with which he set out—he even tells Belle he wishes O'Malley had escaped before they crossed the border. But love drastically complicates the issue. At a party given by Belle, Missy appears in a dress worn by her mother many years previously; O'Malley recognizes the dress and also finds himself drawn to the beautiful girl. The passionate Missy is determined to win O'Malley and he can no longer resist her. The following morning he tells Belle he intends to take Missy away with him. Painfully she explains why he can't—he's her father. The shattered O'Malley now makes a final decision. He forces a showdown with Stribling and the lawman shoots and kills him. Then, bending over the dead O'Malley he picks up his gun and finds it empty.

The Last Sunset is a strange mixture of conventional and unusual material. Filmed entirely in Mexico, the film lacks impact and Dalton's sadly fanciful O'Malley belongs in a worthier vehicle. As do the well researched bits of western lore, such as a wild range cow having to have its legs roped before it can be milked, and mules being used to pull wagons instead of horses. In one especially interesting scene Stribling explains to Missy how to save a motherless calf—by breathing into its nostrils and thereby giving the animal a sense of association, causing it to follow the person doing the breathing. In a moonlit scene, O'Malley points out that the moonlight glittering

With Carol Lynley

phosphorescently on the shiny horns of the cattle is the rare "St. Elmo's fire." In another scene he gently picks up a bird's nest and gives it to Missy, offering her, on this and other occasions, bits of blarney-like observations about life. Unfortunately, the moments of knowledge and character are spaced out by dull stretches and unconvincing situations.

With Regis Toomey, Dorothy Malone and Carol Lynley

With Christine Kaufmann

Town Without Pity

1961 A Mirisch Production, *in association with* Gloria Films (Munich), *distributed by* United Artists. *Produced and directed by* Gottfried Reinhardt. *Written by* Silvia Reinhardt *and* Georg Hurdalek, *based on the novel* The Verdict *by* Manfred Gregor. *Photographed by* Kurt Hasse. *Edited by* Hermann Haller. *Art director,* Rolf Zehetbauer. *Musical score by* Dimitri Tiomkin. *Running time:* 105 minutes.

CAST: Kirk Douglas *(Major Steve Garrett),* Christine Kaufmann *(Karin Steinhof),* E. G. Marshall *(Major Jerome Pakenham),* Robert Blake *(Jim),* Richard Jaekel *(Bidee),* Frank Sutton *(Chuck),* Mal Sondock *(Joey),* Barbara Ruetting *(Inge),* Hans Nielsen *(Herr Steinhof),* Karin Hardt *(Frau Steinhof),* In-grid Van Bergen *(Trude),* Gerhardt Lippert *(Frank Borgmann),* Eleanore Van Hoogstratten *(His Mother),* Max Haufler *(Dr. Urban),* Siegfried Schurenberg *(Burgermeister),* Rose Renee Roth *(Frau Kulig),* Alan Gifford *(Gen. Stafford).*

Town Without Pity is an odd film. A German-American production about a sex crime committed by American soldiers in Germany, it attempts to philosophize about the disparity between justice and the law, but it reaches no conclusions other than those known by all since the beginning of time—that humans are full of faults like narrow-mindedness and pettiness, and that the law is malleable. The film also ends in a manner that shows no one, German or American, in a particularly kind light.

The setting is a small west German town called

With Richard Jaekel, Robert Blake, Frank Sutton and Mal Sondock

DEFENSE COUNSEL

With Barbara Ruetting

Neustadt. On a summer afternoon, four G.I.'s in civvies wander aimlessly through the countryside, drinking as they go. They appear to be plain, ordinary fellows: Jim (Robert Blake), Bidie (Richard Jaeckel), Chuck (Frank Sutton), and Joey (Mal Sondock). In the woods they spot a pretty and full-bodied sixteen-year-old girl, Karin (Christine Kaufmann), wearing a brief bikini. With Karin is her boyfriend, Frank (Gerhardt Lippert), who is hesitant in his love making, to the chagrin of the sensual Karin. She taunts him about his restraint and he leaves. Shortly afterwards, the four G.I.'s surround the girl, who instantly gathers their intent and recoils from the idea.

Karin's father, Herr Steinhof (Hans Nielsen), together with the town Burgermeister, approaches the local U.S. Army commander and lodges a charge of rape. Outraged, Steinhof demands that the death penalty be imposed; the officer then explains that this will only be possible if Karin takes the witness stand and testifies directly against the men. The four G.I.'s are arrested and the Army brings in an experienced lawyer, Major Steve Garrett (Kirk Douglas), to handle their defense. In moving around Neustadt, Garrett finds himself an unwanted guest. An attractive German newspaperwoman, Inge (Barbara Ruetting), hounds him but soon finds him to be a decent-minded man, intent on doing his job impartially.

Garrett goes to see Karin's parents and explains to them his sympathy and his revulsion at the crime, but he also warns them that if Karin is put on the stand, it will mean a cross-examination that will be painful, unrelenting and possibly injurious to the girl. The morally adamant father will not be swayed in his clamor for justice. Garrett, in questioning townspeople, learns that the pretty Karin is sexually precocious and that she has on occasion been guilty of exposing herself at the window of her bedroom. Garrett feels more and more uneasy about his job but he has no course but to continue.

At the trial Garrett uses the testimonies of the pious citizens to get across an impression of Karin as a tease. He gets a very nasty implication from the mother (Eleanore Van Hoogstratten) of Karin's boyfriend Frank, who suggests the girl has tried to lead her son astray. With Karin on the stand, Garrett lacerates the girl. He accuses her of standing nude in the woods to excite Frank, and that she was in this condition when approached by the G.I.'s. After being badgered in this manner, Karin collapses. Unable to complete her testimony, the death sentence cannot be invoked and the soldiers are then given prison terms. Garrett, far from pleased with himself, prepares to leave town as quickly as possible. As he packs his bags he learns that Karin, ridiculed by the townspeople, has committed suicide. Given the cold shoulder by his fellow officers and jeered at by the townspeople, Garrett leaves Neustadt.

Town Without Pity is an interesting picture but it falls short of its pretentiously moral mark. Neither

With Eleanore Von Hoogstratten

the characters nor the issues come as sharply into focus as they should. This may possibly have something to do with the differences in humor, in viewpoints and in story-telling techniques between the Germans and the Americans involved in the production. In a sense, the film is more fascinating sociologically than cinematically. However, it does give Kirk Douglas a chance to shine as a courtroom lawyer, an opportunity that rightly belongs to every actor at some time in his career. Douglas' performance here is restrained, his Garrett is a compassionate man but frightening when moved to anger. In the courtroom scenes Douglas is matched with a skillful adversary, in both the legal and the histrionic sense—prosecutor E. G. Marshall. In the difficult role of the sensual but sensitive Karin, Christine Kaufmann is excellent. The production values of the film are competent, and inferior in only one area—musical scoring. Surprisingly this is the work of Dimitri Tiomkin, whose rock-and-rollish title song blares from the soundtrack, and the theme of which is repeated ad nausem. Tiomkin has since declared himself not responsible for the manner in which his music was used in the film.

With E. G. Marshall, left, and Christine Kaufmann seated at right

Lonely Are the Brave

1962   A Joel (Kirk Douglas) Production *for* Universal-International. *Produced by* Edward Lewis. *Directed by* David Miller. *Written by* Dalton Trumbo, *based on the novel* Brave Cowboy *by* Edward Abbey. *Photographed by* Phil Lathrop. *Edited by* Leon Barsha. *Art directors,* Alexander Golitzen *and* Robert E. Smith. *Musical score by* Jerry Goldsmith. *Running time:* 107 minutes.

CAST: Kirk Douglas *(Jack Burns),* Gena Rowlands *(Jerri Bondi),* Walter Matthau *(Sheriff Johnson)* Michael Kane *(Paul Bondi),* Carroll O'Connor *(Hinton),* William Schallert *(Harry),* Karl Swenson *(Reverend Hoskins),* George Kennedy *(Gutierrez),* Dan Sheridan *(Deputy Glynn),* Bill Raisch *("One Arm"),* William Mims *(1st Deputy in Bar),* Martin Garralaga *(Old Man),* Lalo Rios *(Prisoner).*

Lonely Are the Brave touched several sensitive areas of the mass psyche when it was first shown in 1962: the desire to be an individual—fear of technology and of the computerized state—contempt for organized society—the slipping away of old values, like manliness and self-respect. And it is a film that will touch the same areas even more acutely with the passing of time. *Lonely Are the Brave* is the story of a cowboy trying to live by his own code, trying not to buckle down to civilization but eventually being beaten by it.

It is one of the films of which Kirk Douglas is most proud, and since it was his own production he deserves credit for having the courage to make a film that had little chance of being a box office winner. It was clearly a role for which he had genuine compassion and as more than one critic has pointed out, Douglas is at his best when *being* someone rather than *acting* a part. And there is also a parallel between Douglas and the loner cowboy of this film— Douglas has always been a maverick movie star,

With Bill Raisch (right)   With Bill Raisch

thumbing his nose at studio contracts and organizing his own film projects, but whereas the cowboy of *Lonely Are the Brave* is a loser, Douglas has so far been able to play the game of individualism with success.

Lonely Are the Brave, astutely scripted by Dalton Trumbo, picks an obvious example to make the point of man's plight in the mechanized world—the beloved American cowboy, roaming the handsome, spacious West in the company of just one companion, his horse. The film opens with such an image; as Douglas lies resting in the empty landscape, clearly content with his freedom, he hears the roar of a jet plane and looks up at it with amused indifference. The plane has no significance for the cowboy but it is a symbol in the story line.

The cowboy visits his friends (Michael Kane and Gena Rowlands) in nearby Albuquerque and finds his friend jailed on a charge of helping in the illegal entry of Mexicans into the United States. Acting like a cowboy in an old movie, Douglas starts a brawl in a saloon in order to get himself arrested and thrown into jail, his object being to free his friend in a break-out. But he finds, a note of signs of changing times, that his happily married friend would rather serve his sentence than risk becoming a fugitive. So Douglas breaks out alone and heads for the hills. That the spunky loner must be captured and brought to justice becomes the painful duty of a compassionate sheriff, played laconically and humanely by Walter Matthau. The sheriff of *Lonely Are the Brave* becomes the

conscience of the audience—he sympathizes with the cowboy, he admires his courage but he knows the anachronistic adventurer must be brought into line: "Either you go by the rules or you lose." Reluctantly the sheriff pursues the cowboy and his horse, but despite a jeep and radio communications, and the

With Gena Rowlands

With Michael Kane

bumbling efforts of an army helicopter (there's a moment of triumph for the cowboy when he cripples the flying machine with his rifle) the cowboy makes his way through the mountains and escapes. But there is no lasting escape. During a late and rainy night, the cowboy tries to cross a superhighway; his horse shies at the noise and the lights of speeding vehicles, and within the space of a few moments, horse and rider are felled by a huge diesel truck.

Lonely Are the Brave is a simple story, tautly directed by David Miller, for whom this is a peak in an otherwise not very distinguished career, and it is aided by the sharp, clear photography of Phil Lathrop and an astringent musical score by Jerry Goldsmith. However, it is not a perfect film and critic Stanley Kauffmann raised a valid point: "The film's basic shortcoming is its lack of a desirable alternative to what it seemingly deplores. Many of us uncharmed by neon and motels do not long for the old-time saloon binges and fist fights as the lost Eden." The

With Gena Rowlands

With George Kennedy

question remains unanswered: how do we keep order without smothering the self-reliance of the individual?

The hero of *Lonely Are the Brave* is, apparently, admirable from a distance but a bit of an embarrassment up close. That might be an added reason for the film being a favorite with students at cinema courses in many colleges and universities. It is a film whose style and construction is worthy of examination but it is also a commentary aligned with the feelings of many young people disdainful of contemporary life. Kirk Douglas is aware of this reaction and pleased by it, "It happens to be a point of view I love. This is what attracted me to the story—the difficulty of being an individual today. Life gets more and more complex and convoluted. Young people are not happy with what's going on—and they're right. The character in *Lonely Are the Brave* had that quality. He didn't want to belong to this day and age. It's difficult to buck the system. That's the tragedy of it."

With Edward G. Robinson

Two Weeks in Another Town

1962   An MGM Picture. *Produced by* John House-man. *Directed by* Vincente Minelli. *Written by* Charles Schnee, *based on the novel by* Irwin Shaw. *Photographed in MetroColor by* Milton Krasner. *Edited by* Adrienne Fazan *and* Robert J. Kern, Jr. *Art directors,* George W. Davis *and* Urie McCleary. *Musical score by* David Raksin. *Running time:* 106 minutes.

CAST: Kirk Douglas *(Jack Andrus),* Edward G. Robinson *(Maurice Kruger),* Cyd Charisse *(Carlotta),* George Hamilton *(Davie Drew),* Dahlia Lavi *(Veronica),* Claire Trevor *(Clara),* James Gregory *(Brad Byrd)* Rosanno Schiaffino *(Barzelli),* Joanna Roos *(Janet Bark),* George Macready *(Lew Jordan),* Mino Doro *(Tucino),* Stefan Schnabel *(Zeno),* Vito Scotti *(Assistant Director),* Tom Palmer *(Dr. Cold Eyes),* Erich von Stroheim, Jr. *(Ravinski),* Leslie Uggams *(Chanteuse).*

With Dahlia Lavi

With George Hamilton and Joanna Roos

Two Weeks in Another Town is an attempt to reprise, in a similar vein, the success of *The Bad and the Beautiful*. The same major talents—Kirk Douglas, producer John Houseman, director Vincente Minnelli, scenarist Charles Schnee, and composer David Raksin—rejoined forces for this effort but the results fell sadly short of their previous collaboration. Based on Irwin Shaw's novel about the problems and tensions of creative artists, this screen treatment never quite comes into convincing focus. Again, as in other films about filmdom, the view in bleak; the characters are parasitic, ranting and as despicable as they are complex.

The town of the title is Rome, where much of the film was made. To town comes Jack Andrus (Douglas), formerly a popular film actor but for the last three years an inmate in a sanitarium, the victim of alcoholism and a mental breakdown—also the survivor of a car crash, which leaves him with a thin scar across his face. In Rome he joins director Maurice Kruger *(Edward G. Robinson)* who offers him a small part in a film he is making. Kruger needs help; his film is running behind schedule because of an actress, Barzelli (Rosanna Schiaffino), who barely speaks English, and a leading man, Davie Drew (George Hamilton), who openly despises the director and refuses to take his part seriously.

With Cyd Charisse

The director persuades Andrus to take over the difficult job of supervising the dubbing of the disastrous film. The day before he is due to start, he meets a beautiful Italian girl, Veronica (Dahlia Lavi), whose quiet charm Andrus finds helpful in this frenetic atmosphere. The same evening he also happens to run into his ex-wife, Carlotta (Cyd Charisse), a spoiled, destructive woman, largely responsible for his previous spiritual and professional decline. She is determined to prove she still has a hold on him. The dubbing sessions progress painfully, with Andrus trying to get the best performances from his actors while striving not to return to alcohol. But as he sees more and more footage of the film, he realizes it is a lost cause. The picture is a stinker, or so he thinks.

At a party Kruger gives for his wife, Clara (Claire Trevor), she publicly accuses him of having an affair with his leading lady, Barzelli. A few hours later, the harried director is stricken with a heart attack. Kruger now begs Andrus to take over the film and finish it. Andrus rises to the challenge—directing the remaining scenes and retaking some of the previous ones, cajoling and squeezing good work from his actors. Andrus saves the picture but he finds little appreciation from the egocentric Kruger.

However, Andrus is now a man in control of himself. He has regained his strength and his self-respect, he is free of Kruger and Carlotta and their like. His agent telephones him with an offer to direct a new film but he refuses, deciding instead to take things

easy and accept smaller jobs until he feels truly capable of directing a major film. With the gentle Veronica, he looks forward to a bright future. Two weeks in Rome have enabled him to find himself.

Two Weeks in Another Town lacks conviction, too many of its characters are caricatures. It's most interesting sequence is footage taken from *The Bad and the Beautiful,* a sequence in which the director and the star look back on one of their former triumphs. Unfortunately it serves only to show how much more interesting the former film was, compared to the one in which it is being shown. The main theme of David Raksin's score is sad and haunting, and it serves to illuminate the febrile state of mind of poor Andrus. Raksin also incorporates his marvelous main theme from *The Bad and the Beautiful,* skillfully pointing up the film-within-the-film. Also on the credit side: Milton Krasner's color photography of Rome, a definite asset to the enterprise.

Both Vincente Minnelli and Kirk Douglas admit the film was a disappointment, yet they feel it would have had greater impact had it not been badly re-edited at MGM at the command of a high ranking executive. Says Douglas, "It seems this gentleman decided to supervise the editing himself, putting lines from one scene into another, trying to soften the picture and make it more marketable for the family

trade. It just wasn't that kind of a story. Ironically, this same gentleman left the studio not long after. But by then it was too late to do anything about *Two Weeks in Another Town.*"

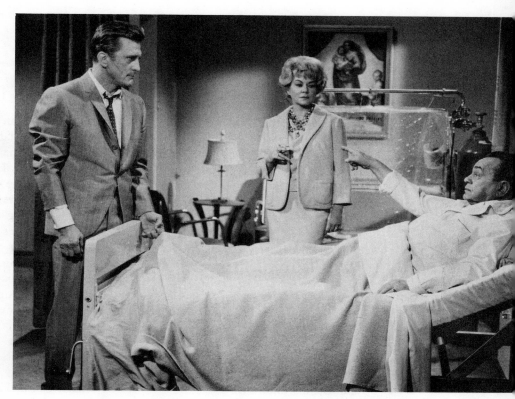

With Claire Trevor and
Edward G. Robinson

The Hook

1963 A Perlberg-Seaton Production, *distributed by* MGM. *Produced by* William Perlberg. *Directed by* George Seaton. *Written by* Henry Denker, *based on the novel* L'Hamecon *by* Vahe Katcha. *Photographed by* Joseph Ruttenberg. *Edited by* Robert J. Kern, Jr. *Art directors,* George W. Davis *and* Hans Peters. *Musical score composed and played by* Larry Adler. *Running time:* 98 minutes.

CAST: Kirk Douglas (*Sgt. P. J. Briscoe*), Robert Walker (*Pvt. O. A. Dennison*), Nick Adams (*Pvt. V. R. Hackett*), Enrique Magalona (*The Prisoner*), Nehemiah Persoff (*Capt. Van Ryn*), Mark Miller (*Lt. D. D. Troy*), John Bleifer (*Steward*).

The Hook is an interesting minor film, an off-beat morality tale that brings the issue of wartime killing down to a dramatic hypothesis: can three soldiers carry out an order to kill a prisoner once they have spent some time with the man and get to know him? Although it is well staged and convincingly acted, the issue is not big enough in scope to fill almost one hundred minutes of screentime. It would have fared much better in the framework of a one-hour television presentation.

The story begins on a beach in Korea in 1953, as a group of American soldiers prepare to evacuate. As they destroy their equipment and vehicles, a North Korean bomber attacks and kills all but three of the men—a tough, hard-nosed sergeant (Kirk Douglas), a Pfc who is the sergeant's flunky (Nick Adams), and a sensitive, idealistic private (Robert Walker). In making their way in a landing craft, from

With Nick Adams, Robert Walker
and Enrique Magalona

the beach to a supply freighter standing by, they pick up a North Korean airman, floating unconscious in the sea. Douglas is all for leaving him but Walker pulls the man from the water and persuades the others to take him aboard the ship. Once aboard, the captain (Nehemiah Persoff) tells them the prisoner will have to share a cabin with the three captors.

The sergeant attempts to contact his base in order to report his position but the only officer he is able to reach is a wounded South Korean major who explains that it is useless to bring the prisoner in because the Korean civilians will kill him—they have just suffered a brutal bombing and many civilians have died. The major orders the sergeant to kill his prisoner. The sergeant, a veteran rounding out twenty years service before retiring on a pension, winces at the instruction but accepts it. His companions are even more concerned, especially Walker, who refuses to

With Robert Walker

With Enrique Magalona, Nick Adams and Robert Walker

With Robert Walker and Nick Adams

obey the sergeant's order to execute the Korean.

The point of *The Hook* is hooked on this slight premise: will the captors be able to bring themselves to shoot the captive? To flesh out the screenplay, the film delves into the characters of the American soldiers. The sergeant is revealed to be a lonely man, reference is made to his not receiving mail, and he balks at answering a question about the place from which he comes. Apparently he is homeless, and as ruthless as he is rootless. The Pfc is a shallow, boot-licking type, held under the sergeant's thumb and made servile by the sergeant's withholding of information concerning the Pfc's dereliction of duty. Young Walker, greatly resembling his late, tragic actor father, is quite simply a civilized, decent-minded man responding to the situation as most people would like to feel they would respond.

Most of the film wobbles as it protractedly weighs its moral. The prisoner, unable to speak or understand English, suffers quiet agonies as he watches the men argue, flounder and fight over his fate. The film picks up some momentum at the end when the terrified prisoner unties the rope that ties him to his cot and makes his way into the cargo hold of the freighter. As he does this, the soldiers learn from the radio that an Armistice has been declared. They rush to free their prisoner but find they must now pursue him to tell him what has happened. The prisoner, unable to understand their yells, assumes the worst and pre-

With Nick Adams

pares to protect himself. In so doing, he is accidentally killed.

The Hook lacks dramatic substance, and it is weakened by platitudinous dialogue. It is saved from boredom only by its fine actors, especially Enrique Magalona as the suffering prisoner—a performance with barely a word spoken—by Persoff as a worldly, humane ship's captain, and by Douglas as a soldier whose glib hardness hides an empty heart. He is not a likable man but Douglas makes him familiar and understandable.

For Love or Money

1963   A Universal Picture. *Produced by* Robert Arthur. *Directed by* Michael Gordon. *Written by* Larry Marks *and* Michael Morris. *Photographed in Eastmancolor by* Clifford Stine. *Edited by* Alma Macrorie. *Art directors,* Alexander Golitzen *and* Malcolm Brown. *Musical score by* Frank De Vol. *Running time:* 108 minutes.

CAST: Kirk Douglas *(Deke Gentry)*, Mitzi Gaynor *(Kate Brasher)*, Gig Young *(Sonny Smith)*, Thelma Ritter *(Chloe Brasher)*, Leslie Parrish *(Jan Brasher)*, Julie Newmar *(Bonnie Brasher)*, William Bendix *(Joe Fogel)*, Richard Sargent *(Harvey Wofford)*, William Windom *(Sam Travis)*, Elizabeth MacRae *(Marsha)*, William Sage *(Orson Roark)*, Ina Victor *(Nurse)*, Alvy Moore *(George)*, Jose Gonzales Gonzales *(Jaime)*, Don McGowan *(Gregor)*, Billy Halop *(Elevator Operator)*, Joey Faye *(Male Shopper)*, Theodore Marcuse *(Artist)*, Frank Mahony *(Red Beard)*.

With Mitzi Gaynor, Leslie Parrish and Julie Newmar

With Thelma Ritter

Dramatic actors stick their necks out whenever they appear in comedies, and for some perverse reason the comedic material they choose to deliver is invariably poor. *For Love or Money* is, unfortunately, a case in point. At best it is a mild farce, at worst it is unbelievably unbelievable. The problem of the extremely wealthy seldom make for sympathetic amusement and *For Love or Money* bears heavily in asking its audience to believe that a super-rich matriarch

would need to hire a matchmaker to find husbands for the like of Mitza Gaynor, Leslie Parrish, and Julie Newmar.

Kirk Douglas appears as a corporation lawyer, a slick, glib playboy-type lawyer whose income tax declarations report his expenses as more than his earnings. Questioned about this he archly rationalizes, "Nobody can help being poor but its criminal to stay poor." But nothing that happens to him in this film is any indication of ability; instead the story is a triumph for his female employer (Thelma Ritter) and her oldest daughter (Mitza Gaynor), who confuse and outwit him at every turn. *For Love or Money* has lawyer Douglas the victim of far too many long-arm coincidences.

As the film opens, Ritter hovers over Douglas' ketch in a helicopter and through a loudspeaker commands him to appear in her office immediately. Douglas turns the sail-boat around and heads for the city. There he is assigned to manage the estates of widow Ritter's three rebellious daughters, one of whom is bright and capable but two of whom are lovely numbskulls—Parrish a patron of mod-freakish artists, and Newmar a fanatic on physical culture. After a while Douglas is informed by Ritter that part of his job is to find suitable husbands for her daughters—and to see that the job is carried out without hanky-panky, she assigns her hotel-chain chief of detectives (William Bendix) to dog his every move. Douglas manages to land a meek income tax clerk (Richard Sargent) for Newmar and a prison instructor (William Windom) for Parrish. For Gaynor he tries to line up dates with a playboy-millionaire, who is always too busy with other young ladies to turn up,

With Gig Young and Julie Newmar

With Mitzi Gaynor

thus causing Gaynor to suspect Douglas is either incompetent or trying to make out with her himself. The role of the millionaire—a hopelessly improbable characterization—is played by Gig Young, in the light-hearted, light-headed, constantly tipsy style for which he has become familiar. Desperately tired of playing such silly parts, Young finally received recognition, and an Oscar, for his acting ability in *They Shoot Horses, Don't They?* (1969).

The frantic complications of *For Love or Money* subside when Douglas and Gaynor discover they love each other. The two other daughters settle for their Douglas-picked mates and the film ends with a triple wedding. One of the funnier moments of the whole enterprise is the last one, as Bendix pays off a wager to Ritter that the girls would end up married, the biggest part of the wager being that Gaynor would get Douglas. Thus Mama turns out to be the real matchmaker.

Kirk Douglas was not pleased with the outcome of the picture but he could only have been confused with the extreme diversity of the comments of two esteemed critics. Said Bosley Crowther: "Witless nonsense. Douglas' way with a *bon mot* or a little comedy twist is to have at it pugnaciously." Said Judith Crist: "Kirk Douglas proves himself an expert with a fast line and a comic situation."

With Mitzi Gaynor and Gig Young

The List of Adrian Messenger

1963   A Joel (Kirk Douglas) Production, *distributed by* Universal. *Produced by* Edward Lewis. *Directed by* John Huston. *Written by* Anthony Veiller, *based on the novel by* Philip MacDonald. *Photographed by* Joseph MacDonald. *Edited by* Terry Morse *and* Hugh Fowler. *Art directors,* Alexander Golitzen, Stephen Grimes *and* George Webb. *Musical score by* Jerry Goldsmith. *Running time:* 98 minutes.

CAST: George C. Scott *(Anthony Gethryn)*, Dana Wynter *(Lady Jocelyn Bruttenholm)*, Clive Brook *(Marquis of Gleneyre)*, Herbert Marshall *(Sir Wilfred Lucas)*, Jacques Roux *(Raoul Le Borg)*, Bernard Archard *(Inspector Pike)*, Gladys Cooper *(Mrs. Karoudjan)*, Walter Anthony Huston *(Derek)*, John Merivale *(Adrian Messenger)*, Marcel Dalio *(Max)*, Anita Sharpe-Bolster *(Shopkeeper)*, Noel Purcell *(Farmer)*, John Huston *(Huntsman)*, *and* Kirk Douglas *(George Brougham)*. *Guest stars:* Tony Curtis, Burt Lancaster, Robert Mitchum, *and* Frank Sinatra.

The idea of using several famous Hollywood actors in heavily disguised bit parts obviously seemed an excellent commercial gimmick at the outset of production on *The List of Adrian Messenger*, but it was an expensive idea that largely backfired. To those moviegoers fascinated by playing such a guessing game, and those interested in the skill of makeup expert Bud Westmore, the idea had some entertainment value, but to those looking to director John

Huston for a sharp tale of crime and detection, it was an irritant. For the record: Frank Sinatra, Burt Lancaster, Tony Curtis, and Robert Mitchum appear as a gypsy, a ban-the-fox-hunt matron, an organ grinder, and a crippled pensioner. At the end of the film they pop up in an epilogue and remove their Westmore putty-masks. Kirk Douglas also appears in disguise in the picture but he is an integral character in the story, and he is seen manipulating his disguises.

Anthony Veiller wrote a taut screenplay based on the popular Philip McDonald thriller, and it is excellently cast and directed by Huston, who skillfully uses English and Irish locations. Huston, long an Irish resident, knows much about the personality of the British landed gentry, especially the Irish aristocrats' love of fox hunting and this knowledge gives his picture an extra shine. It begins at a tea party on the estate of the Marquis of Gleneyre—played by Clive Brook, coaxed out of a long retirement by John Huston to play the role of the feisty old clan chieftain. A retired British intelligence officer, Anthony Gethryn (George C. Scott), is given a list of eleven names by his friend Adrian Messenger, one of the Gleneyres (John Merivale), and asked by him to check the whereabouts of the people listed. As Gethryn proceeds with his investigation, Messenger is the victim of a sabotaged airliner which explodes and crashes

in the ocean. Messenger and a survivor are seen clinging to a piece of wreckage, with Messenger mumbling information before he dies.

The survivor is Raoul Le Borg (Jacques Roux), a French industrialist but formerly a wartime espionage

With Dana Wynter, George C. Scott and Clive Brooks

With Walter Anthony Huston

With George C. Scott

agent with a knowledge of explosives and a trained memory. He is also, it turns out, a man well known to Gethryn, and the two men unite to crack the mystery. Le Borg confirms that the airplane was the object of a bombing, due to the smell of cordite, and he recalls the jumbled words of Messenger. Their sleuthing gradually narrows the case down; all the names on the Messenger list are dead, all the victims of seeming accidents, and all were at one time P.O.W.'s in Burma. The man responsible for the killings was himself a P.O.W. and an informer who revealed the escape plans of his comrades. He is also a member of the Gleneyre family—George Brougham, born in Canada and the son of the Marquis' long lost brother.

John Huston lets his audience in on the mys-

tery fairly early in the picture. Kirk Douglas, as Brougham, is seen in several disguises as he accounts for various victims. Brougham's master plan is to inherit the vast Gleneyre estate and fortune; the eighty-year-old Marquis will have to name an inheritor—his twelve-year-old grandson, Derek (Walter Anthony Huston, son of the director). The boy is finally all that stands between Brougham and the inheritance, as Gethryn and Le Borg are now well aware. They move to the Gleneyre estate to keep an eye on the boy, and so does Brougham, who arrives and makes himself known to his great-uncle. Brougham is a debonair gentleman and he charms his relatives with tales of his adventures, and his cattle ranch in Canada.

Gethryn asks Brougham's advice on a murder mystery he is trying to solve, deliberately letting slip a little incriminating information, and setting himself up as the next victim. Brougham later tells his hosts he must go to London on business for a day or so and begs to be excused. Now he sets a trap, taking a fox in a sack and dragging it across fields to a high stone wall, on the other side of which he places a large, heavily spiked ploughing machine. He thus wagers on Gethryn, usually the lead horseman in the fox hunts, being the first over the wall.

The following day, the fox hunt takes place but it ends with the death of George Brougham, now disguised as an old farmer. Gethryn removes the ploughing machine but he stands at the wall with a dog and halts the hunt. He knows the dog will lead

With director John Huston

him to the culprit, standing amid the crowd of spectators. As the dog nears, Brougham makes a run to get away, he takes Derek's horse and tries to leap the wall but Derek calls to his horse as it is about to jump—it stalls and Brougham is pitched over the wall, landing on the spikes of the ploughing machine moved by Gethryn. It is a horribly ironic end—as well as improbable that Brougham should be pitched at that particular spot—and as he lays dying he partly pulls away his disguise.

The List of Adrian Messenger is a good, slick item of its kind, although somewhat impaired by its gimmickry. John Huston's direction is tight and bright, but one suspects his main interest in doing the picture was the opportunity to stage several elaborate fox hunting sequences in County Wicklow, a sport at which he is an *aficionado*. Huston also appears as one of the aristocratic riders, giving himself one line of dialogue. His son, Walter Anthony, rides the hunt with a skill that suggests he shares his father's interests. Kirk Douglas, whose company produced the film, clearly enjoyed himself playing the villain with a genius for disguises. For George C. Scott the role of the intelligence officer was a relatively easy assignment, although, as critic Stanley Kauffmann pointed out, in his scenes with such grand English types as Clive Brook, Herbert Marshall, and Gladys Cooper, "he sounds about as English as Nelson Rockefeller." The film also gets solid aid from composer Jerry Goldsmith, his music is eerie in its macabre moments and suitably rollicking in the extensive and well-filmed fox hunting sequences.

During the making of *The List of Adrian Messenger;* Douglas arrived home one evening in one of the disguises used in the film. He fooled everyone except his wife, Anne. With them are their sons Peter and Eric

With Burt Lancaster

Seven Days in May

1964   A Seven Arts-Joel Production, *distributed by* Paramount. *Produced by* Edward Lewis. *Directed by* John Frankenheimer. *Written by* Rod Serling, *based on the novel by* Fletcher Knebel *and* Charles W. Bailey. *Photographed by* Ellsworth Fredericks. *Edited by* Ferris Webster. *Art director,* Cary Odell. *Musical score by* Jerry Goldsmith. *Running time:* 120 minutes.

CAST: Burt Lancaster *(Gen. James M. Scott),* Kirk Douglas *(Col. Martin Casey),* Fredric March *(President Jordan Lyman),* Ava Gardner *(Eleanor Holbrook),* Edmond O'Brien *(Sen. Raymond Clark),* Martin Balsam *(Paul Girard),* George Macready *(Christopher Todd),* Whit Bissell *(Sen. Prentice),* Hugh Marlowe *(Harold McPherson),* Bart Burns *(Arthur Corwin),* Richard Anderson *(Col. Murdock),* Jack Mullaney *(Lt. Hough),* Andrew Duggan *(Col. "Mutt" Henderson),* John Larkin *(Col. Broderick),* Malcolm Atterbury *(White House Physician),* Helen Kleeb *(Esther Townsend),* John Houseman *(Admiral Barnswell),* Collete Jackson *(Bar Girl).*

Kirk Douglas has often said that if a film has a message it should be well couched in the form of entertainment. *Seven Days in May* is a precise illustration of that dictum. The message here is a big one: beware the military-industrial complex. It is a meaty issue and the film tackles it in no half-hearted fashion.

With Burt Lancaster

With Richard Anderson

Seven Days in May is a suspense story, skillfully paced and acted out by thorough professionals, and the fact that it deals intelligently and calmly—and nonpropagandistically—with politically relevant fears, gives it a disturbing fascination.

John Frankenheimer had just previously directed a politically orientated mystery movie, the superb *The Manchurian Candidate,* in which a Communist brainwashed assassin eliminates a fascistic contender for the White House, and in *Seven Days in May* he steered a story about a possible overthrow of the government by a military putsch. Both films were risky topics as movie entertainment and both needed the commitment of big-name actors before money could be raised. It was the sanction of Frank Sinatra that enabled *The Manchurian Candidate* to move into production and it was the enthusiasm of Kirk Douglas, who acquired the rights to the novel by Fletcher Knebel and Charles W. Bailey, that initiated the birth of *Seven Days in May*. Douglas and his producer-partner Edward Lewis were able to enlist the interest of Burt Lancaster once John Frankenheimer was signed to direct; the young (then thirty-three) director had guided Lancaster through *The Young Savages* and *Birdman of Alcatraz* and was highly regarded by the difficult-to-impress actor. To strengthen the bid for financing, Douglas and Lewis added the prestigi-

With Edmond O'Brien, and Fredric March

ous Fredric March to the cast and brought Ava Gardner back to Hollywood for the first time in half a dozen years. Then, with a tight budget of $2,200,000 they set about telling a tale many American film producers would not have chosen to touch:

The President of the United States, despite the advice of his military advisors, concludes a nuclear treaty with Russia. To his chief of staff (Lancaster) this is considered stupid and almost treasonable. Some time later, a marine colonel on his staff (Doug-

With Martin Balsam and Fredric March

With Martin Balsam

las) comes across information that points to the existence of a secret military base somewhere in the wilds of the southwest. His suspicions grow as he hears mysterious messages being passed between Lancaster and other high-ranking officers. Douglas deduces the planning of a coup and he reports his fears to the president. A trusted senator (Edmond O'Brien) is sent to investigate, and when he discovers the base he is held prisoner, until brought out at gunpoint by an officer friend of Douglas. A presidential aide is next sent to Gibraltar to force information from a conspiring admiral but the aide is killed in an air crash on the way back to Washington. A devious and distasteful means is next employed as Douglas visits the former mistress (Ava Gardner) of the chief of staff and steals some incriminating letters that could, if necessary, be used as blackmail. The president and the chief of staff confront each other but the president cannot bring himself to use the letters. Instead he addresses the nation and calls for the resignation of the guilty officers, most of whom desert Lancaster when it becomes known that the admiral's statement has been found in the wreckage of the aide's plane. The coup dissipates and dies.

Seven Days in May has a chilling, ominous atmosphere. It is realistically staged and frighteningly plausible. Frankenheimer gives the picture a documentary look, filling it with military, governmental, and technological detail, so that the fantasy appears factual. Much of the exteriors were filmed in Washington. In his book on Frankenheimer, Canadian film critic Gerald Pratley quotes the director:

> We did not ask the Pentagon for co-operation because we knew we wouldn't get it. But there was no active resistance to it. I'm sure the Pentagon weren't happy when they heard we were going to make it but at the same time they didn't try to

With Richard Anderson and Burt Lancaster

With Ava Gardner

With Ava Gardner

With director John Frankenheimer, Fredric March and Martin Balsam

censor us. I heard that President Kennedy, indirectly (I never had the pleasure of meeting him personally) said he very much wanted the film made. Pierre Salinger, who was then his Press Secretary, was very helpful to us and when we shot the White House scenes he arranged for the President to go to Hyannisport. Now if the White House had not wanted the film made I can assure you that we could not have obtained permission to shoot a small riot in front of it. Pierre Salinger was also very gracious, taking us through the President's office and other rooms so that we could copy them accurately in the studio.

The performances of Lancaster, Douglas and March account for a great deal of the film's effectiveness. Lancaster's chief of staff is a dedicated man, not a traitorous man, and his quiet, glacial playing of the part makes it uncomfortably believable. Fredric March appears as a dignified but ailing president, courageously summoning the strength to maintain his station. But it is Douglas who has the most difficult part, that of an honest and patriotic man who feels morally bound to report a possible insurrection, the lack of which will present him as a meddling fool and the presence of which will force him into the obnoxious duty of an informer. Douglas plays the sometimes painful part of the catalyst of *Seven Days in May* in a manner more subdued and restrained than most of his film performances. The style contributes to the sharpness of this stinging picture.

With Jill Haworth

In Harm's Way

1965   A Sigma Production, *distributed by* Paramont. *Produced and directed by* Otto Preminger. *Written by* Wendell Mayes, *based on the novel by* James Bassett. *Photographed by* Loyal Griggs. *Edited by* George Tomasini *and* Hugh S. Fowler. *Art director,* Al Roelofs. *Musical score by* Jerry Goldsmith. *Running time:* 165 minutes.

CAST: John Wayne *(Capt. Rockwell Torrey),* Kirk Douglas *(Cdr. Paul Eddington),* Patricia Neal *(Lt. Maggie Haynes),* Tom Tryon *(Lt. [jg] William McConnel),* Paula Prentiss *(Bev McConnel),* Brandon De Wilde *(Ens. Jeremiah Torrey),* Jill Haworth *(Ens. Annalee Dorne),* Dana Andrews *(Adm. Broderick),* Stanley Holloway *(Clayton Canfil),* Burgess Meredith *(Cdr. Powell),* Franchot Tone *(CINCPAC I Admiral),* Patrick O'Neal *(Cdr. Neal Owynn),* Carroll O'Connor *(Lt. Cdr. Burke),* Slim Pickens *(CPO Culpepper)* James Mitchum *(Ens. Griggs),* George Kennedy *(Col. Gregory),* Bruce Cabot *(Quartermaster Quoddy),* Barbara Bouchet *(Liz Eddington),* Tod Andrews *(Capt. Tuthill),* Larry Hagman *(Lt. Cline),* Stewart Moss *(Ens. Balch),* Richard Le Pore *(Lt. Tom Agar),* Chet Stratton *(Ship's Doctor),* Soo Young *(Tearful Woman),* Dort Clark *(Boston),* Phil Mattingly *(P-T Boat Skipper),* Henry Fonda *(CINCPAC II Admiral).*

War, it is often said, brings out the best and the worst in man. A similar observation might be made about those who produce films about war. Stanley Kubrick clearly saw *Paths of Glory* as a trenchant comment on men exposed to hideous circumstances. Otto Preminger apparently looked upon *In Harm's Way* as an opportunity to serve up almost three hours of gargantuan entertainment. To Preminger's credit, this film is much more pithy and pungent than most other films that have dealt with naval warfare in the Second World War. With skill and gall, and a dubious taste that has made him controversial and popular,

With John Wayne

Preminger here spaced his moments of heroism with insights into cowardice and opportunism and stupidity in high naval places, adding incidents dealing with adultery, rape, suicide and generation gap.

If Kirk Douglas was able to make Colonel Dax a thoroughly believable and admirable man, he could do nothing with his role as Commander Paul Eddington except stride with the hokum and employ the bravura style he uses when tackling shallow characterizations. Commander Eddington is none too believable and far from admirable: he is a cuckolded hero whose pretty young wife is killed in the bombing of Pearl Harbor. His feelings of bitterness grow and fester, and in a plot device that is not as plausibly written as it need be, he rapes a young, virginal nurse (Jill Haworth), the girl friend of an Ensign (Brandon De Wilde), who happens to be the son of his boss (John Wayne). Later, presumably rotten with

With John Wayne

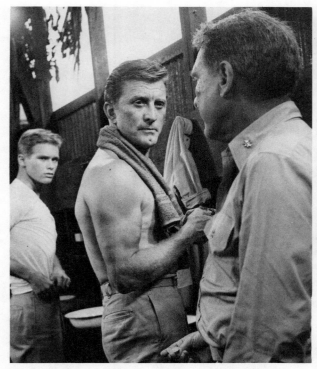

With Jill Haworth and Patricia Neal

guilt and cynicism, he commandeers an airplane and sacrifices himself by flying over the Japanese fleet and reporting their location.

Kirk Douglas carried off this faintly absurd mixture of heroics and soap opera with the expertise born of twenty years before the cameras. But *In Harm's Way* is not a Douglas film, it is a John Wayne epic, through which the huge veteran trundles like a Rock of Gibraltar on wheels. As a naval captain who fails his first assignment in the Pacific immediately after the Pearl Harbor attack he is pulled off the ocean and put in charge of a desk. His capabilities are gradually recognized; he is put in charge of an important naval campaign and brings it off successfully. For Wayne the part was almost tailor made, and well within his leathery reach.

Pointing only to the melodramatics of *In Harm's Way* is unfair to Preminger. The long picture moves fairly swiftly and the battle scenes are well paced, although the battleships are too obviously models in tanks. Filming the story on location in Hawaii was an asset and there is a vitality to the depiction of naval life. Especially commendable is the casting in this film: Patricia Neal as a nurse who loves and marries Wayne is especially effective—truly a Woman, mature and understanding; Burgess Meredith as a

With Patrick O'Neal and Brandon De Wilde

sardonic wartime officer and a peacetime film writer, contributes moments of sane observation, particularly in a scene with Wayne discussing fear. Henry Fonda plays a firm and capable admirable, Dana Andrews plays a weak and not very capable admiral, and Franchot Tone appears as a knowledgeable, political type of admiral, each actor giving *In Harm's Way* its badly needed touches of credibility. But the Preminger picture will never turn up on anyone's list of Great War Movies, and Kirk Douglas' role in it will not be one by which he will be remembered.

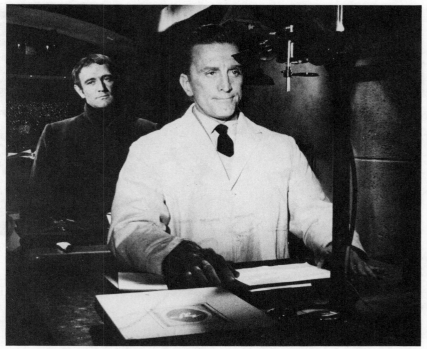

With Richard Harris

The Heroes of Telemark

1965   A Benton Film Production, *distributed by* Columbia Pictures. *Produced by* S. Benjamin Fisz. *Directed by* Anthony Mann. *Written by* Ivan Moffat *and* Ben Barzman, *based on* Skis Against the Atom *by* Knut Haukelid, *and* But For These Men *by* John Drummond. *Photographed in Technicolor by* Robert Krasker. *Edited by* Bert Bates. *Art director,* Tony Masters. *Musical score by* Malcolm Arnold. *Running time:* 131 minutes.

CAST: Kirk Douglas *(Dr. Rolf Pedersen),* Richard Harris *(Knut Straud),* Ulla Jacobsson *(Anna),* Michael Redgrave *(Uncle),* David Weston *(Arne),* Anton Diffring *(Major Frick),* Eric Porter *(Terboven),* Mervyn Johns *(Colonel Wilkinson),* Jennifer Hilary *(Sigrid),* Roy Dotrice *(Jensen),* Barry Jones *(Professor Logan),* Ralph Michael *(Nilssen),* Geoffrey Keen *(General Bolts),* Maurice Denham *(Doctor at Hospital),* Wolf Frees *(Knippelberg),* Robert Ayres *(General Courts),* Sebastian Breaks *(Gunnar),* John Golightly *(Freddy),* Alan Howard *(Oli),* Patrick Jordan *(Henrik),* William Marlowe *(Claus),* Brook Williams *(Einar),* David Davies *(Captain of the Galtesund),* Karel Stepanek *(Hartmuller).*

The Heroes of Telemark was the last complete film by director Anthony Mann. He died two years later, in 1967, while working on *A Dandy in Aspic.* Mann was especially gifted in filming exteriors, in a sense he was a landscape artist, and *The Heroes of Telemark* is a fairly routine war adventure story greatly enhanced by Mann's sweeping vistas of Norway in winter. Mann directed eight of the best James Stewart westerns, all of them marked by a sensitive sense of the spectacular, and in 1961 he moved to Europe to make the impressive *El Cid.* He spent his

With Richard Harris

With Ulla Jacobsson

remaining years in Europe, directing the visually interesting but otherwise disappointing *The Fall of the Roman Empire* and then this expensive British picture about the men who crippled the German atomic research efforts in Norway during the Second War War.

Public acceptance of *The Heroes of Telemark* fell sadly short of expectations. This is regrettable because the film was handsomely produced and it told a true story of an interesting and commendable enterprise. But by the mid-1960's the public appetite for war films was limited to those that were blackly humorous or bizarre or those carrying a definite anti-war message. A straightforward account of a bold adventure found limited favor, yet to have filmed *Telemark* as anything other than straightforward would have been impossible since many Norwegians who participated in the actual wartime operation lent their services to the making of the picture.

The Heroes of Telemark used actual locations to relate how Norwegian Resistance fighters prevented the Germans from securing a key ingredient needed

With Mervyn Johns, Robert Ayres, Geoffrey Keen and Richard Harris

for their atomic research—"heavy water." Kirk Douglas plays Dr. Rolf Pedersen, the Oslo University scientist who first recognized the significance of German heavy water production at the fortified factory in Rjukan, and Richard Harris appears as a tough, winter sportsman, underground leader. The dissimilar men, somewhat at odds according to this screenplay, combined their efforts to defeat the Germans. Part of the film was made in England but the company spent two months in the winter of 1964–1965 in Norway, filming in sub-zero temperatures but achieving, with the aid of ace British cinematographer Robert Krasker, some stunning footage. The company hired Norwegian skiing champions to coach the actors and Olympic coach Helge Stoylen actually carried a Panavision camera between his legs during swift passages over the snows and brought in some remarkable shots. The Norwegian co-operation was, in Douglas' opinion, of a kind seldom encountered.

An essential element in the production of the film was obtaining permission from the Norsk Hydro Company to some sites of the story, from the Vemork factory to the railway ferry on Lake Tinnsjo. The company was able to use the remarkable exterior of the factory, set on a rocky cliffside, and because part of the factory was being renovated it was also able to shoot inside. Mann and his crew were lucky in being able to use a ferry ship of the same kind used during the war, and Lt. Col. Knut Haukelid of the Norwegian Army, who participated in the actual wartime operation, was contracted as technical adviser. It was therefore possible to give *The Heroes of Telemark* a remarkable verisimilitude.

The plot centers on the two raids made by the Norwegians against the German atomic program, the first, on February 27, 1943, consisted of nine men breaking into the factory and destroying the atomic equipment, and the second, on February 20, 1944, when just two men sank the ferry boat taking a shipment of heavy water to Germany. The Norwegians were thus able to do what British Commandos and American bombers had not been able to do—foil the German efforts to create the atomic bomb.

Cast a Giant Shadow

1966   A Mirisch-Llenroe-Batjac Production, *distributed by* United Artists. *Produced, directed and written by* Melville Shavelson, *based on the book by* Ted Berkman. *Photographed in DeLuxe Color by* Aldo Tonti. *Edited by* Bert Bates *and* Gene Ruggiero. *Art director,* Arrigo Equini. *Musical score by* Elmer Bernstein. *Running time:* 141 minutes.

CAST: Kirk Douglas *(Col. David "Mickey" Marcus)*, Senta Berger *(Magda Simon)*, Angie Dickinson *(Emma Marcus)*, James Donald *(Safir)*, Stathis Giallelis *(Ram Oren)*, Luther Adler *(Jacob Zion)*, Gary Merrill *(Pentagon Chief of Staff)*, Haym Topol *(Abou Ibn Kader)*, Ruth White *(Mrs. Chaison)*, Gordon Jackson *(James MacAfee)*, Michael Hordern *(British Ambassador)*, Allan Cuthbertson *(British Immigration Officer)*, Jeremy Kemp *(Senior British Officer on the beach)*, Sean

Barrett *(Junior British Officer on the beach)*, Michael Shillo *(Andre [Magda's Husband])*, *and* Frank Sinatra *(Vince)*, Yul Brynner *(Asher Gonen)*, John Wayne *(Gen. Mike Randolph)*.

With John Wayne

With Allan Cuthbertson, James Donald and Senta Berger

To those who were involved in its production *Cast a Giant Shadow* is referred to as Cast a Giant *Shudder*. The mishaps were so numerous and the difficulties so picaresque that its producer, Melville Shavelson, who also directed and wrote the script, later made it the subject of a book called *How To Make a Jewish Movie*. If Shavelson elects to make a film of this book it might well emerge as a comic masterpiece, al-

though it is safe to assume that nothing is likely to persuade Shavelson to make another epic dealing with the founding of Israel—if it is to be filmed in Israel. Shavelson's book clearly points to the endless problems involved in making a large-scale film on a foreign location, particularly if it is a location in a country populated by individualists. Film making calls for precise co-operation and co-ordination. Shavelson's adventures in Israel provided him with endless material for humorous anecdotes but not enough material to make a memorable film. A point in the actual screenplay illustrates Shavelson's operation in Israel: Kirk Douglas, in leading a military maneuver against the Arab Legion, orders his officers to synchronize their watches for the attack. They thereupon admit they don't have watches. According to Shavelson this incident was not untypical of his general campaign in Israel filming *Cast a Giant Shadow*.

The pity is that the film had a genuinely heroic story to tell. Its subject is Colonel David "Mickey" Marcus, an American with a distinguished record as a lawyer and as a soldier, who was persuaded by the Israeli Government in 1947 to organize and command an army to defend the country from the Arabs after the British withdrawal from Palestine. Marcus did, in fact, build an army from the rag-tag militia of Israel and managed to combine two diverse forces—the Haganah, the underground fighters, and the

With Angie Dickinson, John Wayne
and Michael Hordern

With Yul Brynner, Senta Berger
and Stathis Giallelis

Palmach, the youthful commando force. After Marcus' death, his widow received a letter from David Ben Gurion in which she was told, "He was the best man we had."

The failure of *Cast a Giant Shadow* was in its conception. Shavelson, a veteran and astute moviemaker, realized the difficulty of raising backing for a project about the man who raised the Israeli Army, and he was compelled to popularize the picture, adding romantic angles and bringing in name "guest stars" in the form of John Wayne and Frank Sinatra. It was necessary, it seems, to present Marcus as a crusading daredevil, the kind of man who could not be deterred from the challenge of destiny, even by a beautiful wife—vivified by Angie Dickenson. The film added a fictional romance with a luscious lady freedom-fighter, a fantasy fleshed out by Senta Berger—Vienna's answer to Sophia Loren. Such ploys are often necessary to fund films, but in this instance, coupled with the problems of a difficult location, they

With Luther Adler

With Senta Berger

fortune, throwing seltzer bottles from his plane while flying over Egyptian tanks, contributed only absurdity.

Nonetheless, *Cast a Giant Shadow* deserved a better reception than it received. The long film contained many interesting vistas of Israel, and the story of the incredible Marcus and his part in the fight to establish a new nation should have brought wider attention. Kirk Douglas, a past master at delineating determination, was able to communicate Marcus' love of tackling seemingly impossible assignments. In flashback sequences the film showed moments of Marcus' involvement in the Second World War, and in one especially ironic scene he is decorated by the British Ambassador for services rendered in the war and then gently warned by the representative of the Crown that they are aware of his activities in Palestine.

Cast a Giant Shadow touches on many Israeli ironies, the most memorable, and the saddest, being the death of "Mickey" Marcus. He was shot dead by one of his own sentries on the night before the truce with the Arab Nations that brought about the independence of Israel. Marcus died because he could not speak Hebrew and could not understand the challenge of his sentry.

backfired. The addition of glamour fictionalized what should have been a near-documentary and the presence of Frank Sinatra, in a cameo role as a pilot-of-

Is Paris Burning?

1966   A Transcontinental Films-Marianne Production, *presented by* Paramount-Seven Arts-Ray Stark, *distributed by* Paramount. *Produced by* Paul Graetz. *Directed by* Rene Clement. *Written by* Gore Vidal *and* Francis Coppola, *based on the book by* Larry Collins *and* Dominique Lapierre. *Photographed by* Marcel Grignon. *Edited by* Robert Lawrence. *Art directors,* Willy Holt *and* Roger Volper. *Musical score by* Maurice Jarre. *Running time:* 165 minutes.

CAST: *(in alphabetical order):* Jean-Paul Belmondo *(Yvon Morandat),* Charles Boyer *(Dr. Monod),* Leslie Caron *(Francoise Labe),* Jean-Pierre Cassel *(Lt. Henri Karcher),* George Chakiris *(G.I. in Tank),* Alain Delon

(Gen. Jacques Chaban-Delmas), Kirk Douglas *(Gen. George S. Patton)*, Glenn Ford *(Gen. Omar Bradley)*, Gert Frobe *(Gen. Dietrich Von Choltitz)*, E. G. Marshall *(Powell)*, Yves Montand *(Bizien)*, Anthony Perkins *(Warren)*, Simone Signoret *(Café Proprietress)*, Robert Stack *(Sibert)*, Marie Versini *(Claire)*, Skip Ward *(G.I. with Warren)*, Orson Welles *(Swedish Consul Nordling)*.

The most admirable thing about *Is Paris Burning?* is the effort that went into making it. That the city of Paris in the summer of 1965 could actually be used as the setting of a war film employing a huge cast and crew is little short of amazing. By dint of much time and superhuman patience the producers managed to get the co-operation of the French Army, various agencies of the French Government, and the many ministries of Paris to recreate the liberation of the French capitol by the Allied Armies and the French underground forces in 1944. Even allowing for the fervor of Parisian pride, the logistics involved in stag-

ing the events of twenty-one years previously—using the actual locations—were staggering. Areas of the city had to be blocked off for hours at a time, mostly between five in the morning and noon, with director Rene Clement dividing his team into units and shooting sequences in several locations simultaneously. When it was impossible to get any more footage on the actual locations, Clement had replicas built at the French Army base at Satory, near Versailles. Equally admirable were the efforts that went into combing Europe for period military material—tanks, jeeps, trucks, guns, etc.—and putting them into the hands of thousands of extras. However, it must be noted, with an inevitable touch of black humor, that producer Paul Graetz died only a matter of weeks after the cameras ceased turning on his massive project. The heart attack suffered by the sixty-five-year-old producer might well have been brought on by the strain of making *Is Paris Burning?*

Unfortunately, Graetz' last picture turned out to be a mind-boggling mess. It is too inaccurate to be a documentary and too confusing to be good entertainment. The admirable book by Larry Collins and Dominique Lapierre defied a literal filming. Packed with complicated situations and shallow characterizations, *Is Paris Burning?* almost needs a chart to follow. Especially confusing are the attempts the film makes to tell the story from many angles—Allied,

Gert Frobe as Dietrich Von Choltitz

German and French, with the French motivations de-
fying all but the experts. On one particular issue, *Is
Paris Burning?* is contemptible: it depicts the late
Dietrich Von Choltitz as a rather heartless soldier
who somehow never got around to obeying Hitler's
orders to destroy Paris whereas, in fact, the German
commander deliberately evaded the orders in order to
save the city.

Is Paris Burning? indulges in the dubious practice
of bolstering its box office appeal with famous film
stars in cameo roles. The reason is obviously commercial; the producers of expensive epics assume that
the public will be attracted to see their favorites doing
bits. In most cases it has been a policy that has backfired. Mike Todd made it work for *Around the World
in Eighty Days* because each cameo was brightly
written and performed and contributed to the story
line. On the other extreme, George Stevens destroyed
the credibility of *The Greatest Story Ever Told* by
sprinkling it with familiar faces—the end result was
like a religious vaudeville revue. In the case of *Is
Paris Burning?* the appearance of several famous stars
in small parts detracted from the film's pretentions of
documentary style. Kirk Douglas appears as Lt. Gen.
George S. Patton, to whom the French Underground
forces send an envoy in an appeal for help. Patton
tersely explains he is not in the business of liberating
cities but he passes the envoy to another officer who
might, and does, help. The Douglas cameo as Patton
serves no real purpose; not because the part is not

With Pierre Vaneck

convincingly played but because the actor is not on
screen long enough to establish a characterization
and overcome the impression of a movie star appearing as a guest. In this peculiar situation a star is at a
disadvantage. Producers had best give such bits to
unfamiliar actors and not interrupt the plausibility of
their stories.

With Pierre Vaneck

The Way West

1967   A Harold Hecht Production, *distributed by* United Artists. *Produced by* Harold Hecht. *Directed by* Andrew V. McLaglen. *Written by* Ben Madlow *and* Mitch Linderman, *based on the novel by* A. B. Guthrie, Jr. *Photographed in Deluxe Color by* William H. Clothier. *Edited by* Otho Lovering. *Art director,* Ted Haworth. *Musical score by* Bronislau Kaper. *Running time:* 122 minutes.

CAST: Kirk Douglas *(Senator William J. Tadlock)*, Robert Mitchum *(Dick Summers)*, Richard Widmark *(Lije Evans)*, Lola Albright *(Rebecca Evans)*, Michael Witney *(Johnnie Mack)*, Sally Field *(Mercy McBee)*, Katherine Justice *(Amanda Mack)*, Stubby Kaye *(Sam Fairman)*, William Lundigan *(Michael Moynihan)*, Paul Lukather *(Turley)*, Roy Barcroft *(Masters)*, Jack Elam *(Weatherby)*, Patric Knowles *(Col. Grant)*, Ken Murray

With Richard Widmark and Lola Albright (in wagon), Robert Mitchum and Michael McGreevey (behind Douglas)

(Hank), John Mitchum *(Little Henry),* Nick Cravat *(Calvelli),* Harry Carey, Jr. *(Mr. McBee),* Roy Glenn *(Saunders),* Michael McGreevey *(Brownie Evans),* Connie Sawyer *(Mrs. McBee),* Anne Barton *(Mrs. Moynihan),* Eve McVeagh *(Mrs. Masters),* Peggy Stewart *(Mrs. Turley),* Stefan Arngrim *(Tadlock, Jr.).*

The Way West might well have emerged as a classic western. Based on the Pulitzer Prize winning novel by A. B. Guthrie, Jr., it is the story of a large band of pioneers who leave Independence, Missouri, in 1843 and follow the Oregon Trail to the fabled northwestern land of promise. More than five million dollars was spent making the film, but the filmic trip is a lumpy one and the end result is a massive disappointment. The characterizations are routine, the direction limp and too many of the incidents are dubious in intent and not sufficiently motivated. What saves *The Way West* from being a total cliché are some handsome production values and many magnificent locations filmed in Oregon.

The role played by Kirk Douglas is full of potential but it is betrayed by poor scripting. His Senator William J. Tadlock is a visionary, a dedicated leader who organizes the Oregon Liberty Company and in-

361.   With Robert Mitchum and Richard Widmark

spires a group of emigrants to follow him in his plans to build new cities in the far off paradise. Douglas easily conveys the persuasiveness and fanaticism of such a man, an inspiring figure but also a man whose obsession has driven his wife to suicide and who could well become a demagogue when his dream project is realized.

The film begins with an admirable facsimile of the Independence of 1843, a town packed with eager emigrants, itching to be off on the way west. The scenes are remarkable in conveying the dress and manners and accouterments of the period. The pioneers are a wide assortment of types, mostly family people, and the film shines in those moments when it explores the growing excitement of the impending trip, and then shows the start of the trek; wagons, carriages, horses, oxen, cattle and people struggling through the muddy streets and heading into the unknown. Few films have depicted such scenes better than this. Other highlights are those that show the difficult fording of rivers by the wagon train and the painful progress across desert country and through snowy mountains.

The Way West suffers from trying to tell too many stories in its two hours; too many of the pioneers are complicated people rather than ordinary folk. Richard Widmark and Lola Albright appear as a married couple, not quite united on his passion to head west; their teenage son (Michael McGreevey) falls for a sexy young girl (Sally Field), but she flirts with, and is eventually raped by, a frustrated young farmer (Michael Witney) whose frigid wife has problems not made clear by the script. Some animosity builds between Douglas and Widmark when there is the hint of desire in the leader's glances toward the other man's wife. Robert Mitchum, looking understandably bored, is the veteran trail scout, persuaded against his better judgment to lead the party through the wilderness.

With Lola Albright and Richard Widmark

Indians appear in *The Way West,* as they have every right to appear. Their involvement in the plot is more interesting than the usual device of Indians hampering the pioneers. At one point Mitchum rescues young McGreevey from a Sioux scouting party, at the cost of several barrels of whisky. Later, when the Indians visit the camp in search of more to drink, the drunken Witney seduces the teasing Sally Field and then takes a shot at what he thinks is a wolf, although it happens to be an Indian boy hiding in a wolf skin. Sometime later the Indians catch up with the wagon train and demand retribution, whereupon Tadlock ceremoniously hangs Witney, causing a certain measure of disgust among the pioneers, particularly the hanged man's frigid wife. Tragedy soon strikes at Douglas when his young son is killed in a buffalo stampede. Feeling he must be punished Douglas orders his Negro slave to flog him with a whip; this is a poorly concocted scene and smacks more of masochism than righteous self-control. It is one of a number of scenes in *The Way West* that make the long trek as uncomfortable for the audience as the pioneers.

Gradually the feeling of his followers turn against Douglas; as the hardship of the long trip bears down on them they find his discipline uncompromising and cruel. He certainly is not a man to be deflected from his course; when the wagon train rests at a fort and tastes a little rest and relaxation, some of the pioneers speak of quitting, whereupon Douglas reports a false case of smallpox in his train, causing an immediate dismissal of the entire company from the fort. As the pioneers become more tired so Douglas becomes more obsessed. Finally they revolt and Widmark takes over as leader. Then, while making a descent by rope down a steep gorge, the once frigid wife, now a hateful widow, cuts the rope and Douglas plunges to his death. Sobered by his death, the pioneers vow to complete the trek as he planned it.

As a travelogue *The Way West* is worthy of close attention. Most of the exteriors were shot in Oregon and handsomely lensed by the veteran cinematographer William H. Clothier, whose previous assignment had been *Shenandoah* and who would next work on *The War Wagon.* His Deluxe Color-Panavision framing of *The Way West* makes the lack of a good script and solid direction all too regrettable. Points of visual interest: the river crossing scene was staged

With Stefan Arngrim

near Willamette, sixteen minutes from Eugene; the sequence with the buffalo herd was shot on the Ponderosa Ranch, thirty-five miles each of Burns; the desert crossing was photographed on the dunes of Shifting Sands, fifty miles east of Fort Rock; the mountain crossing was staged on the 7700-foot crest of Mount Bachelor; and other scenes were filmed at the Crooked River Gorge, and on the Deschutes and Willamette Rivers. In many instances the locations were as much an unspoiled revelation to the film's cast and crew as the Oregon Trail must have been to the pioneers of 1843. If nothing else, *The Way West* is a splendid introduction to Oregon.

With Robert Mitchum, Richard Widmark, Michael McGreevey and Lola Albright

The War Wagon

1967   A Batjac-Marvin Schwartz Production, *distributed by* Universal-International. *Produced by* Marvin Schwartz. *Directed by* Burt Kennedy. *Written by* Clare Huffaker, *based on his novel* Badman. *Photographed in Technicolor by* William H. Clothier. *Edited by* Harry Gerstad. *Art director,* Alfred Sweeney. *Musical score by* Dimitri Tiomkin. *Running time:* 101 minutes.

CAST: John Wayne *(Taw Jackson),* Kirk Douglas *(Lomax),* Howard Keel *(Levi Walking Bear),* Robert Walker *(Billy Hyatt),* Keenan Wynn *(Wes Catlin),* Bruce Cabot *(Pierce),* Valora Noland *(Kate),* Gene Evans *(Hoag),* Joanna Barnes *(Lola),* Bruce Dern *(Hammond),* Terry Wilson *(Strike),* Don Collier *(Shack),* Sheb Wooley *(Snyder),* Ann McCrea *(Felicia),* Emilio Fernandez *(Calita),* Frank McGrath *(Bartender).*

The War Wagon is not nearly as ambitious a western as *The Way West* but it is more enjoyable because it has no pretensions. It is a fictional romp with no roots in reality. It has nothing to do with the history of the American West, only that never-never adventure land invented by Hollywood. John Wayne strides through the picture as his usual growling, lovable bear-like self, but *The War Wagon* shows Kirk Douglas off to advantage in a lusty, athletic performance as a gun-for-hire rogue. Douglas twirls six-guns with the skill of a juggler, leaps railings and vaults onto horses with a physical exuberance that belies his fifty years.

The vehicle of the title is an armored stagecoach, mounted with a Gatling gun, and owned and operated by crooked Bruce Cabot. Clair Huffaker's screenplay, based on his novel *Badman,* makes no bones about its characters, many of whom are robbers and the rest of whom are on the side of justice only if the price is right. They follow their paths for reasons of gain. John Wayne is a man out for revenge; framed

With John Wayne

and sent to jail by Cabot, a crooked mine owner who takes over the Wayne home and land, he returns to claim his rights. Douglas, a stylish gunman, had been hired by Cabot to kill Wayne prior to the imprisonment but failed to do so. Now he is offered $12,000 to complete the job; instead he forms an alliance with Wayne to seize and rob the iron-plated wagon and share its wealth, presumably gold bullion worth hundreds of thousands of dollars. They round up a gang of odd characters, including an alcoholic young explosives expert (Robert Walker), a mordantly humorous Indian (Howard Keel), and a mean old codger (Keenan Wynn) with a pretty young wife (Valora Noland). Since the wagon is always heavily guarded and escorted, as well as devilishly armed, the devices to rob it are necessarily ingenious and sometimes hilarious. The film is full of fist fights, frantic chases, barroom antics, and a near-slapstick finale in which the badmen are liquidated, but in which the pursuers fail to fulfill their plans to get rich quick. The real winners become a band of confused Kiowa Indians, into whose unknowing hands the gold falls. The entire caper is carried on with the aid of a thunderous musical score by Dimitri Tiomkin, who when asked how a Russian composer could write such rousing music for westerns, shrugged his shoulders and replied, "A steppe is a steppe is a steppe."

Kirk Douglas had by this time appeared in eleven westerns. As both an entertainer and a businessman he is fully appreciative of the western as a film force. Also, like many actors who play in westerns he enjoys the work. Says Douglas: "No actor I know would

With John Wayne and Howard Keel

With Joanna Barnes

turn down a good role in a western. Practically all of my colleagues, from comedians to the most sophisticated types, are on the lookout for a cowboy flick. They may claim that they want to do one as a change of pace, or a chance to show their versatility. The truth is that they are just as much drawn to the guntoting hero as the child who wants his first present to be a 'hogleg' and holster and cowboy hat. Psychologists try to explain this perpetual enthusiasm for westerns in terms of symbolism. They find in the gun, the horse, the ten-gallon hat and the wide open spaces symbols which are unconsciously significant to an audience. The same story told in different terms wouldn't have the same impact. So say the psychologists, and I suppose their guess is as good as anyone else's. What then, is the secret of the western's appeal? Is it plot? I doubt it. The plot of most westerns is simple. And how many different plots could possibly be contrived for the thousands of westerns that have been filmed over the years? I think the essential appeal lies in the character of the cowboy himself. He is the figure audiences want to identify with. He is the cult idol around whom this whole form of worship revolves."

With John Wayne

A Lovely Way to Die

With Kenneth Haigh

1968   A Universal Picture. *Produced by* Richard Lewis. *Directed by* David Lowell Rich. *Written by* A. J. Russell. *Photographed in Technicolor by* Morris Hartzband. *Edited by* Sidney Katz. *Art director,* Willard Levitas. *Musical score by* Kenyon Hopkins. *Running time:* 103 minutes.

CAST: Kirk Douglas *(Jim Schuyler)*, Sylva Koscina *(Rena Westabrook)*, Eli Wallach *(Tennessee Fredericks)*, Kenneth Haigh *(Jonathan Fleming)*, Martyn Green *(Finchley)*, Sharon Farrell *(Carol)*, Ruth White *(Cook)*, Doris Roberts *(Feeney)*, Carey Nairnes *(Harris)*, John Rogers *(Cooper)*, Philip Bosco *(Fuller)*, Ralph Waite *(Sean Magruder)*, Meg Myles *(Mrs. Magruder)*, Gordon Peters *(Eric)*, William Roerick *(Loren Westabrook)*, Dana Elcar *(Layton)*, Dee Victor *(Mrs. Gordon)*, Dolph Sweet *(Haver)*, Lincoln Kilpatrick *(Daley)*, Alex Stevens *(Lumson)*, Conrad Bain *(James Lawrence)*, Robert Gerringer *(Connor)*, John Ryan *(Harry Samson)*.

A Lovely Way to Die demanded little of Kirk Douglas. He waded through the film like a champion swimmer making a guest appearance at a kiddie pool. The part of a tough, slick, world-weary cop might have been played by any number of Universal's contract players. In point of fact, it is only one of a number of glossy crime movies that studio churned out in the late sixties, movies like *P.J., Madigan,* and *Coogan's Bluff.* Since most of these films used New York City as their setting, and employed the same kind of flashy editing and jazzy music scoring, the films tend to be barely distinguishable one from the other. When *A Lovely Way to Die* was shown on television in early 1972, expunged of a few sexy moments, it had precisely the look of the telefilms Universal was then feeding the networks. In the four years between its theatrical and its television release, the Douglas film had dated in only one regard: as a policeman reputed to be excessively harsh in his treatment of criminals, Douglas appears mild and moderate compared to the brutal policemen depicted in *The French Connection* and *Dirty Harry,* two box office winners of 1971 and 1972. Such "progress" is food for thought.

A Lovely Way to Die is good, lightweight entertainment. Douglas plays a policeman who resigns rather than be called to account for his vicious manner with lawbreakers, handing in his badge with the comment, "I just can't get used to coddling criminals." He is immediately hired by a lawyer (Eli Wallach) as bodyguard to a beautiful and rich young woman (Sylva Koscina) who is accused of murdering her husband, aided by her lover (Kenneth Haigh).

With Sylva Koscina

She is innocent of the charge but seemingly trapped by the mysterious circumstances of the case. When a witness, who could testify that she and her playboy lover were at a scene other than the one of the crime, is murdered, Douglas becomes bent on solving the case. Inevitably he falls in love with the body he has been hired to guard.

The plot is, like other films of this genre, absurdly involved and full of improbabilities. The slain husband loses his life when his car gets stuck in mud on the side of a road and he goes for help at a nearby mansion. There he discovers that the owner of

With Eli Wallach

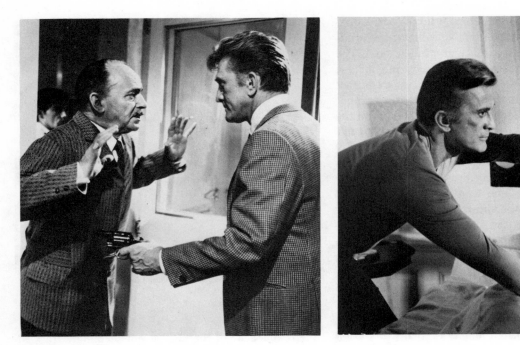

With Martyn Green

With Sylva Koscina

the house has been killed by a gang who intend to take over the estate. The husband is killed in order not to reveal their scheme, and it serves the gang's purpose to let the young widow take the rap for her husband's death.

That Kirk Douglas, or whoever else played the role, could unravel the mystery, nail the wrongdoers, save the girl and have her fly into his arms at the finale is predictable—and expectable. All that matters is style and *A Lovely Way to Die* is not to be taken as anything more than inconsequential entertainment. Douglas helped with his easy but firm playing, nicely matched with the beautiful and saucy Sylva Koscina. Universal brought their film factory expertise to bear, supplying all the right technical skills to turn out a shiny product, although it is debatable that films of this kind need the kind of raucous musical scoring here laid on by Kenyon Hopkins.

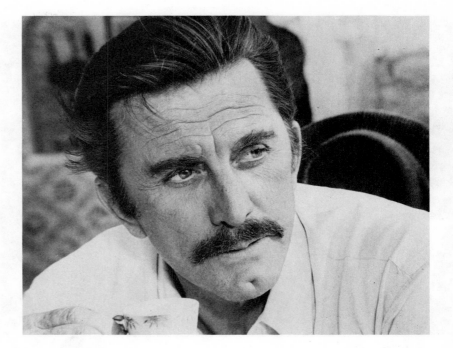

The Brotherhood

1969 A Brotherhood Company Production for Paramount Pictures. *Produced by* Kirk Douglas. *Directed by* Martin Ritt. *Written by* Lewis John Carlino. *Photographed in Technicolor by* Boris Kaufman. *Edited by* Frank Bracht. *Art director,* Tambi Larsen. *Musical score by* Lalo Schifrin. *Running time:* 96 minutes.

CAST: Kirk Douglas *(Frank Ginetta)*, Alex Cord *(Vince Ginetta)*, Irene Papas *(Ida Ginetta)*, Luther Adler *(Dominick Bertolo)*, Susan Strasberg *(Emma Ginetta)*, Murray Hamilton *(Jim Egan)*, Eduardo Ciannelli *(Don Peppino)*, Joe De Santis *(Pietro Rizzi)*, Connie Scott *(Carmelo Ginetta)*, Val Avery *(Jake Rotherman)*, Val Bisoglio *(Cheech)*, Alan Hewitt *(Sol Levin)*, Barry Primus *(Vido)*, Michele Cimarosa *(Toto)*, Louis Badolati *(Don Turridu)*.

With Alex Cord

With Irene Papas

The effort Kirk Douglas puts into his acting often has much to do with his business involvement in a film. *A Lovely Way to Die* is an example of Douglas turning up for work, doing a competent job, and then going home. *The Brotherhood,* on the other hand, represents Douglas the film producer, putting all his effort into a project to make it shine. Unfortunately, the subject matter of this admirably made film is doubtful stuff, dealing as it does with the homelife and internal functionings of the Mafia. No matter how human the hoods are at home and no matter how businesslike their dealings, the film strains the interest and sympathy of the viewer.

The Brotherhood is a commendable piece of film making and it is at its best in delineating the generation gaps within the Mafia. It clearly, and frighteningly, shows the progression from the rough hustlings of old-style gangsters to the cool manipulations of new-style crooks insinuating themselves into Big Business. The film tacitly invites sympathy from the audience for the one style against the other, and in siding with the old rogues, who appear to have all the personality and all the chivalry, however warped, the viewer leaves the picture with a certain confusion, if not guilt.

Douglas appears in *The Brotherhood* as a middle-

With Luther Adler and Joe De Santis

With Eduardo Ciannelli

aged, career crook, born and brought up in the Mafia and dedicated to it. He tells his young brother (Alex Cord), "I was eighteen years old when I had to make my first hit," and he says it with a glow of warm recollection. But he is a gangster bound to the old ways and he opposes the young brother on any plans to tackle new businesses of the Space Age. The brothers clash when syndicate board member Douglas vetoes any involvement that might bring them into conflict with the federal government. When the father-in-law (Luther Adler) of the young brother instigates a move to replace Douglas, an elderly, deposed head of the Mafia (Eduardo Ciannelli) reveals to Douglas that it was Adler who betrayed and caused the massacre of forty top leaders of the previous syndicate, including Douglas' father. Douglas then brutally murders Adler and flees with his wife and daughter to Sicily.

The life of retirement in Sicily comes to an end, as the fatalistic Douglas knows it must, when the young brother arrives for a visit. The older brother realizes that the visit is really an assignment, a "hit," and that the distraught young man must carry it out at the risk of losing his own life and the lives of his family. Douglas makes it easy, he takes the young brother to an almond grove, speaking quietly about

their past, and then hands him a rifle that belonged to their father. Douglas then kisses his brother—the Mafia kiss of death—and asks for the fatal shot. The scene is chillingly matter of fact, with Douglas' chauffeur driving the surviving brother to the airport and sending him on his way, back to the family trade.

The Brotherhood is tough minded and intelligently presented but it suffers from a kind of removed fascination. It is difficult for the noncriminal to empathize with Mafia types, no matter how good they are as family men. It is, nonetheless, an interesting insight into the organized underworld and the film makes a touching statement for the families of these men, especially the wives. Douglas' wife is played by the magnificent Irene Papas, and it is a deep, warm performance of a mature woman.

If Kirk Douglas can be faulted for his performance in *The Brotherhood* it can only be in those moments when his intensity spills over and becomes bombast. Perhaps as the film's producer, obviously concerned to make an exceptional picture, he was unable to contain his considerable vigor. The difficult final scene, however, deserves praise as the work of a skilled screen performer. Douglas also deserves comment for the excellence of the casting, especially

With Alex Cord

the old men who play the Mafia veterans, their hard, sad faces lined like walnut trees. Especially notice-able is Eduardo Ciannelli, here making, in the eighty-second and final year of his life, one of his last appearances before the cameras. Ciannelli had been a character actor in Hollywood for almost forty years and in *The Brotherhood* his leathery, rutted, once-handsome old face looked worthy of chiselling on a Sicilian mountainside.

With Alex Cord

With Elia Kazan

The Arrangement

1969   An Elia Kazan Production, *distributed by* Warner Bros. *Produced, directed and written by* Elia Kazan, *based on his novel. Photographed in Technicolor by* Robert Surtees. *Edited by* Stefan Arnstein. *Art director,* Malcomb C. Bert. *Musical score by* David Amram. *Running time: 125 minutes.*

CAST: Kirk Douglas *(Eddie and Evangelos),* Faye Dunaway *(Gwen),* Deborah Kerr *(Florence Anderson),* Richard Boone *(Sam Anderson),* Hume Cronyn *(Arthur),* Michael Higgins *(Michael),* John Randolph Jones *(Charles),* Carol Rossen *(Gloria),* Anne Hegira *(Thomna),* William Hansen *(Dr. Weeks),* Charles Drake *(Finnegan),* Harold Gould *(Dr. Leibman),* E. J. Andre *(Uncle Joe),* Michael Murphy *(Father Draddy),* Philip Bourneuf *(Judge Morris),* Dianne Hull *(Ellen).*

At the commencement of filming *The Arrangement* Elia Kazan jokingly said to Kirk Douglas, "My life is in your hands." Bearing that in mind, it becomes even harder to understand why the film was such a severe failure at the box office. With Kazan producing and directing his screen treatment of his own best-selling novel, the result of the film is entirely his. Perhaps in dealing with material that he confesses is somewhat autobiographical, Kazan was too close to the project, too deep in the trees to see the forest. Even more surprising, Kazan spent a huge budget, reputedly in the neighborhood of six million dollars, putting on screen what would have been more effective in a modest, economical setting.

The Arrangement is an elaborate parable about the plight of the civilized modern man caught up in the vortex of success. Eddie Anderson (Kirk Douglas) is a brilliant advertising executive who seemingly has everything—affluence, comfort, an expensive home and an understanding wife (Deborah Kerr), in addi-

With Michael Higgins and Deborah Kerr

reviews his life, frequently fantasizing about his mistress, who has left him and now lives with another man. He remembers, not with much sympathy, his tyrannical father (Richard Boone) and his overprotective mother (Anne Hegira), and how they shaped, or misshaped, his life.

Eventually Eddie speaks, he tells his wife, "I don't like my life. I don't like the person I am." His wife tries to help, but her resentment of his mistress keeps coming to mind and undermining her sympathy. He manages to bring himself to resume his work, but he soon flies off the tracks again and almost ruins his company. Now he flees to New York, intent on rescuing his sick old father from the clutches of his doctors, and taking him to the old family house on Long Island. Next Eddie tracks down his mistress in New York and urges her to come and live with him in the house. She, with understandable trepidation, agrees to try the arrangement, to the chagrin of her current lover. Eddie's wife, who has achieved the power of attorney, thanks to the efforts of their family lawyer (Hume Cronyn), descends on the house and has the father returned to the hospital. Eddie goes wild and sets the old house afire, after which he follows his confused and fleeing mistress to her apartment. There, the lover shoots Eddie. Again, he survives, but presses no charges—instead he submits to being committed to an institution. The wife and the mistress now arrive at an uneasy truce, they manage

tion to a lovely mistress (Faye Dunaway). While he appears to have everything, Eddie feels in his heart he has nothing. He finally feels choked with self-disgust—life, he muses, is only a series of arrangements. He tries to commit suicide by crashing his small sports car into a truck but he survives the accident and undergoes a long convalescence. Although he recovers physically, he remains mentally distraught and refuses to talk to anyone. Introspectively, Eddie

With Faye Dunaway

With Faye Dunaway

With Harold Gould and Deborah Kerr

to coax him back to normal life, and together they escort him to his father's funeral.

The Arrangement ends with a freeze-frame shot of Kirk Douglas looking back at his father's grave. His expression suggests some peace of mind and the viewer is left to assume he may have overcome his trauma. But it is a slim assumption and Kazan leaves his audience not only hanging but wondering if any real point has been made in this very long, almost psychiatric examination. Too many loose ends dangle, not the least is whether Eddie is a man worth bothering about. More than one critic has pointed out that *The Arrangement* is an old-fashioned story wrapped up in modish, new-fangled techniques. The failure of the picture can be laid squarely at the feet of Kazan; with a magnificent cast and all the technical expertise big money can buy, he should have been able to tell his story in a more direct manner, instead of such a confusion of convoluted flashbacks. The device of having Eddie visit the scenes of his young years and actually stand aside and watch himself as a boy is better suited to the stage than the screen. Kazan almost sabotages his picture with scenes treated in burlesque style, as when Eddie imagines himself beating up his mistress' new boyfriend—the sequence is handled like a slice of a *Batman* TV episode, with signs of "Pow!" "Zonk!" and "Splat!" punctuating the garrishly colored frames. In another greatly ingenious and expensive segment, tiny bits of indecent photographs of Eddie and his mistress romping nude on a

With Deborah Kerr

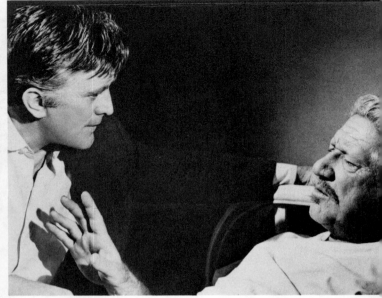

With Richard Boone

beach, come together and come to life, after the wife has torn up the photos and thrown them on the floor. It is terrible and unnecessary wastage of great skills.

To make his film *au courant* commercial, Kazan sprinkles it with strong language and candid sex scenes, none of which help the whole. The pity is that *The Arrangement* might have been a fine essay in

film making; certainly its actors perform with great purpose and ability. Deborah Kerr and Faye Dunaway are touching in their anguish and their efforts to help the man they love, and Richard Boone and Hume Cronyn are perfect as the dotty father and the shrewd lawyer. Kirk Douglas works like a trojan as Eddie; it is a bravura performance, full of energy and subtlety—a complete immersion in a role, regretfully so in view of the end result.

With Hume Cronyn

There Was a Crooked Man

1970   A Warner Brothers-Seven Arts Production. *Produced and directed by* Joseph L. Mankiewicz. *Written by* David Newman *and* Robert Benton. *Photographed in Technicolor by* Harry Stradling, Jr. *Edited by* Gene Milford. *Art director,* Edward Carrere. *Musical score by* Charles Strouse. *Running time:* 126 minutes.

CAST: Kirk Douglas *(Paris Pitman, Jr.)*, Henry Fonda *(Woodward Lopeman)*, Hume Cronyn *(Dudley Whinner)*, Warren Oates *(Floyd Moon)*, Burgess Meredith *(The Missouri Kid)*, John Randolph *(Cyrus McNutt)*, Arthur O'Connell *(Mr. Lomax)*, Martin Gabel *(Warden Le Goff)*, Michael Blodgett *(Coy Cavendish)*, Claudia McNeil *(Madam)*, Alan Hale *(Tobaccy)*, Victor French *(Whiskey)*, Lee Grant *(Mrs. Bullard)*, C. K. Yang *(Ah-Ping)*, Pamela Hensley *(Edwina)*, Bert Freed *(Skinner)*, Barbara Rhoades *(Miss Jessie Brundige)*, J. Edward McKinley *(The Governor)*.

In making *There Was a Crooked Man* Joseph L. Mankiewicz set out with the intention of creating a cynical western, based on the view that there is a little bit of badness even in the best of men. As is often the case in the film industry, the concept is more interesting than the product. What emerges in this long and expert exercise is a film so thoroughly cynical, so negative in its view of the human species that the viewer is allowed no point of view of his own. Only one man in the Mankiewicz picture, the

prison warden played by Henry Fonda, has any moral fiber and even he turns crooked at the very end of the story. For Kirk Douglas, the very crooked man of the title, the film gave scope for bravura playing but the characterization is black and utterly ruthless. Mankiewicz would have done well to ponder the view that there is a little bit of goodness even in the worst of men.

There Was a Crooked Man is admirable in its staging and in the performances of an exemplary cast. Set mostly in a territorial prison in the southwest of the 1880's, Warner Bros. invested $300,000 in building a massive walled prison in the high desert country of the Joshua Tree National Monument, about forty-five miles northeast of Indio, California. Because of helicopter filming, all the fourteen buildings in the set were completely roofed; designed and constructed by Edward Carrere, the prison has a grim sense of reality, so much so that audiences might well believe it to be an actual penitentiary.

There Was a Crooked Man was written by David Newman and Robert Benton, their first script since *Bonnie and Clyde,* but the hand of Mankiewicz is apparent in the interpretation. The witty and civilized

writer-director of *A Letter to Three Wives* and *All About Eve*, both of which brought him Oscars, here overplays his hand in marshaling a ripe and varied group of nefarious characters in an elaborate cobweb of crimes and confidence trickery. Regrettably, the fascinating bits don't add up to a brilliant whole. Douglas, wearing steel-rimmed spectacles and with his hair dyed red, appears at the beginning of the picture as a somewhat cultured bandit; he raids the home of a wealthy rancher and escapes with half a million dollars in cash. In making his escape, several of his men are shot to death and Douglas himself kills his surviving companion. Thus the swag is entirely his. He hides it in a rattlesnake pit in the desert but he is later spotted in a brothel by the rancher and we next see Douglas on his way to jail. In the prison wagon are five fellow felons: Hume Cronyn and John Randolph, a pair of con-men, religious fakers and implicitly homosexual; a huge homicidal Chinaman, played by Olympic athlete C. K. Yang in a screen debut; Michael Blodgett, a young man who accidently killed his girl friend's father when suddenly interrupted in an act of love-making; and Warren Oates, an oafish gunman who shoots sheriff Henry Fonda

With Martin Gabel, Warren Oates, John Randolph, Hume Cronyn, Michael Blodgett and C. K. Yang

With Lee Grant

With Henry Fonda

in the leg when the peaceful, unarmed lawman tries to persuade him to surrender. These endearing rascals are then incarcerated in a cell with a grimy old codger called The Missouri Kid, played like a ferret by Burgess Meredith.

The theme, like that of all prison pictures, is escape, and with Douglas openly boasting of his hidden half-million, escape becomes inevitable and the wily bandit, a born leader of men, can take his pick not only of his accomplices but of the prison warden (Martin Gabel), an effete gentleman, as eager to leave his post as any prisoner. However, a brawl breaks out among the prisoners and in trying to stop it the warden is killed. One irony leads to another and the new warden turns out to be Henry Fonda, a solidly honest, humane man who dedicates himself to penal reform. He quickly spots the officer-like qualities of Douglas and assigns him to supervising the building

With director Joseph L. Mankiewicz
and Henry Fonda

of a new dining hall. It is during the inauguration of the building, attended by the state governor and his guests, that Douglas elects to spark a revolt—his cover for escape.

There Was a Crooked Man is graphic in depicting the sweat and stench of life in a desert prison, and the frustration and despair of its inmates. The spirit of decency, exemplified by Fonda's warden, is almost a jarring note in an atmosphere swirling with resentment and spite. Mankiewicz does not spare the sensitivities of his audience, this is a film about criminals in jail and they do not behave like Boy Scouts at camp. One particular scene, with Douglas besting a bully in a vicious brawl, has him dragging the hapless loser head-first through a trough of urine and then stuffing his head through a toilet hole.

It is the unredeemable quality of Douglas' bandit that undermines the humor of the film. In escaping from the prison he murders the men who have befriended him and helped him escape. His unwillingness to share his illicit fortune makes his death not only unsurprising but unaffecting. Douglas reaches his rattlesnake pit, shoots the snakes and pulls out the package, wrapped in feminine bloomers. Pulling the bundle apart he finds a snake inside. The snake bites him in the neck and within a minute Douglas is

dead, his last word being a common expletive of disgust. Fonda, the pursuer, arrives shortly after and takes the body back to prison but as he is about to ride through the gates he stops. He looks at the bags containing the half million, considers them for a moment and then sends the horse carrying the body into the prison as he himself turns in the opposite direction and rides off to Mexico.

Mankiewicz' film has some memorable moments: Douglas, in his opening robbery, commenting on the excellence of the fried chicken being served at the rancher's table; Hume Cronyn, passing himself off as a deaf mute at a church gathering, backing into a hot stove and yelling a profane curse; a pretty schoolteacher reciting Henley's *Invictus* at the dining room ceremony, watched by hundreds of hungry eyes; and in the elongated chaos of the revolt, a furious montage of incidents, particularly the old Missouri Kid sitting, weeping because he has been in prison too long and hasn't the courage to leave "home," and Cronyn, like a firm-minded old wife, leading his companion back into their cell and telling him they will serve out their sentence. But the sum total of *There Was a Crooked Man* is too much—too mocking, too acid—and the aftertaste is bitter.

A Gunfight

1971   A Harvest-Thoroughbred-Bryna Production, *distributed by* MGM. *Produced by* Ronnie Lubin *and* Harold Jack Bloom. *Directed by* Lamont Johnson. *Written by* Harold Jack Bloom. *Photographed in Technicolor by* David M. Walsh. *Edited by* Bill Mosher. *Art director,* Tambi Larsen. *Musical score by* Laurence Rosenthal. *Running time:* 89 minutes.

CAST: Kirk Douglas *(Will Tenneray)*, Johnny Cash *(Abe Cross)*, Jane Alexander *(Nora Tenneray)*, Raf Vallone *(Francisco Alvarez)*, Karen Black *(Jenny Simms)*, Eric Douglas *(Bud Tenneray)*, Philip Mead *(Kyle)*, John Wallwork *(Toby)*, Dana Elcar *(Mary Green)*, Robert J. Wilke *(Cater)*, George Le Bow *(Dekker)*, Don Cavasos *(Newt Hale)*, Keith Carradine *(Cowboy)*, Paul Lambert *(Ed Fleury)*, Neil Davis *(Canberry)*, David Burleson *(First Poker Player)*, Dick O'Shea *(Second Poker Player)*, Douglas Doran *(Teller)*, John Gill *(Foreman)*, Timothy Tuinstra *(Joey)*, R. C. Bishop *(MacIntyre)*, Donna Dillenschneider *and* Paula Dillenschneider *(Saloon Hostesses)*.

The western remains a staple of the cinema because it is an elemental story structure. It allows for almost any form of human predicament and characterization; it is, in a sense, Greek tragedy played with guns and horses amid handsome, sunny landscapes. Certainly no genre of film has survived so many bad examples or produced more entertainment. *A Gunfight*, hindered by a vague title, is one of the more interesting entries and achieves the near impossible by introducing a fresh theme. It presents the situation of two weary, veteran gunfighters who gamble on the outcome of a contest staged between them in a bullfight arena, with the townspeople gathered as bettors.

The casting of *A Gunfight* is especially good. Kirk Douglas, long experienced with twirling six-guns, plays his has-been hero with a dash of bitterness, a man sick enough of his life to take a double-or-nothing gamble. Johnny Cash, in his first dramatic part, is ideal as a glum, laconic drifter who knows that even

With son Eric

With Jane Alexander

able dance-hall girl adds a little pity to the story by falling in love with Cash while fully realizing he is just another shadow passing through her life. All the characters have a sense of fatalism and it gives *A Gunfight* a poignancy rare in westerns. The film also has a musical score by Laurence Rosenthal that is in itself a rarity—it is subtle and sympathetic and cleverly shades the visual.

The story line of *A Gunfight* has Cash riding into a small town in the southwest because his horse has

if he wins, he will eventually lose. Broadway actress Jane Alexander, as Douglas' wife, is touching as a woman who knows nothing she can do or say will stop him. And Karen Black as a pretty and vulner-

With Karen Black

entire population immediately begin placing bets on the winner of what they assume will doubtless take place. The two men are thus trapped by their own reputations and by their current down-at-heel circumstances. *A Gunfight* is, as so many good westerns are, a morality tale. It is the urge to gamble that brings death to one of the men, ironically the one who instigated the gamble.

Tenneray, sickened by his shallow life, urges the other gunfighter to exploit the situation and stage a gunfight with paid admission, the winner to take all. Reluctantly the tired drifter agrees, although he knows all the odds are against him. Tenneray gets most of the town's bets, particularly after he guns down a young cowboy challenger in the street. But it is not Tenneray who wins in the arena. A single, lightning-fast shot from his opponent kills him and the dazed spectators leave the arena in silence. As the sad winner prepares to mount his horse and ride away, he and Tenneray's wife stare at each other knowingly, each expressionless. Here director Lamont Johnson spoils his picture by engaging in a visualization of the wife's thoughts, with the contest being won by her husband. The sequence is jarringly anti-climactic, and unnecessary. It detracts from the brilliantly filmed confrontation in the bullfight area, a staging that disconcertingly places the two resigned gunmen in the position of animals being slaughtered for the sport. That they are men willing to die for a purse is a chilling comment on humankind, and a memorable moment in a generally admirable film.

been bitten by a rattlesnake. The horse dies and Cash, a famed gunslinger down on his luck, has barely enough money to buy another. His presence is brought to the attention of Will Tenneray (Douglas), a retired gunman, now picking up a small wage as a kind of celebrity in the saloon. The two men are cordial when they meet and both are relieved to know the other has no interest in fighting, even though the

With Johnny Cash

A *Gunfight* was originally set to be filmed in Spain. That it ended up being filmed in the American west is particularly interesting and more than a little ironic. The Jicarilia Apache tribe of New Mexico heard of the plans for the film and asked to meet with Kirk Douglas and his producers. To their surprise and delight they were informed that the Indians were looking for investments; the wealth of the 1800 member tribe had been built from gas and oil lease incomes and deposits of uranium on their reservation lands. Douglas recalls that the deal with the Jicarilia Apache was concluded within one day, with the film to be made in New Mexico and fully financed by them to the tune of two million dollars. When it was pointed out to them that the story was not about Indians, the Apache replied that that was not their concern, they were interested in the film only as an investment.

With Raf Vallone and Johnny Cash

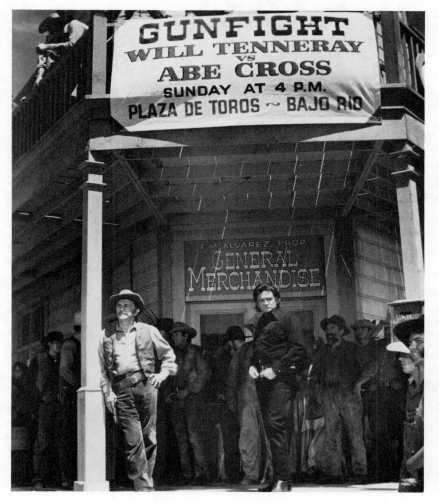

With Johnny Cash

The Light at the Edge of the World

1971 A co-production of Bryna Productions, Inc., Jet Films, S.A. (Spain) *and* Triumfilm (Vaduz), *distributed by* National General Pictures. *Produced by* Kirk Douglas. *Executive Producer,* Alfredo Matas. *Directed by* Kevin Billington. *Written by* Tom Rowe, *based on the novel by* Jules Verne. *Photographed in Eastmancolor by* Henri Decae. *Edited by* Bert Bates. *Art director,* Enrique Alarcon. *Musical score by* Paul Piccioni. *Running time:* 120 minutes.

CAST: Kirk Douglas *(Denton),* Yul Brynner *(Kongre),* Samantha Eggar *(Arabella),* Jean Claude Drouot *(Virgilio),* Fernando Rey *(Captain Moriz),* Renato Salvatori *(Montefiore),* Massimo Ranieri *(Felipe),* Aldo Sambrell *(Tarcante),* Tito Garcia *(Emilio),* Victor Israel *(Das Mortes),* Tony Skios *(Santos),* Luis Barbo *(Calsa Larga),* Tony Cyrus *(Valgolyo),* Raul Castro *(Malapinha),* Oscar Davis *(Amador),* Alejandro de Enciso *(Morabbito),* Martin Uvince *(Balduino),* John Clark *(Matt),* Maria Borge *(Emily Jane),* Juan Cazalilla *(Captain Lafayette).*

A hoary legend of the sea has it that the Atlantic and Pacific Oceans are enemies, and that they meet to do battle at Cape Horn, at the southernmost tip of South America. Certainly it is an area of ferocious seas and badly in need of the lighthouse that the Argentinian government set up in 1865. Seaman refer to the lighthouse as "the light at the edge of the world," a fact that inspired Jules Verne to write a novel with that title, and Kirk Douglas to produce a film from that novel. Douglas, in his constant quest to locate film-funding groups, discovered European backers and co-producers for this venture and proceeded to film the bizarre adventure story on the Spanish coast, near the fishing village of Cadaques, not far from the French border. The location was rugged but much easier to work in than the climatic fury of Cape Horn.

The Light at the Edge of the World is yet another of the many films that have not emerged as their makers had intended. It is basically a pirate yarn but in this filming it is too vicious and bloody for children and too fanciful for adults. Curiously, it suffers from depicting pirates as the cruel, wicked criminals they undoubtedly were, and not the jolly rogues seen in so many previous films of this genre.

The story sets off from an historical fact, that the Argentinian government staffed its lighthouse with three men after its inauguration. According to Verne, they were Moriz (Fernando Rey), an ex-sea captain with a fanatical sense of duty, a young assistant named Felipe (Massimo Ranieri), and an American drifter known as Denton (Kirk Douglas). The American is a man with a mysterious past and, unsuited to the life of a lighthouse keeper, he yearns to get away. Before he gets a chance, a dark, ominous-looking schooner glides into the bay. Moriz and Felipe go to greet it, only to be brutally murdered by its crew. Denton watches in horror and then wisely leaves the lighthouse and hides in a cave. The visitors are pirates, commanded by Kongre (Yul Brynner), a sadistic but cultured brute. The pirates mission is to extinguish the real light and set up their own, in order to lure ships to their doom. When the pirates learn of the existence of Denton, they set about capturing

him. When caught, Denton is humiliated by Kongre but he manages to get away. A further search for Denton is interrupted by a more interesting victim looming into sight—a ship follows the false light and runs aground, whereupon its crew and passengers are horribly put to death. There are two survivors, a beautiful English noblewoman, Arabella (Samantha

Yul Brynner being rowed ashore

With Samantha Eggar

join him. Eventually he is forced to abandon this hope; Kongre orders his men aboard the schooner and turns Arabella over to them for their pleasure, a dreadful deed that inevitably ends in the girl's rape and death. Denton fires at the schooner with a land cannon and blows the vessel to pieces, as Kongre appears at the lighthouse for a hand-to-hand accounting. In their tussle, a shot from the pirate's gun sets the lighthouse afire, and the villain falls burning to his death. Denton is then saved by the ship drawn to the flaming lighthouse, which still glows in the night sky as he leaves.

Rather limply directed, vitiated by its explicit brutality, and weakened by some overly flamboyant acting, especially that of Brynner, *The Light at the Edge of the World* does not shine brightly in the Kirk Douglas catalogue.

Eggar), and the ship's engineer Montefiore (Renato Salvatori). Kongre decides to use the girl as bait to capture Denton; he almost succeeds but Denton again gives him the slip, this time taking Montefiori with him.

The Light at the Edge of the World narrows down to a contest between the American and the pirate leader. Denton becomes determined to end the pirate's career, while the pirate, admiring such courage, hopes to be able to persuade the American to

Catch Me a Spy

1971   A co-production of Ludgate Films (London), Capitole Films (Paris), *and* Bryna, *distributed by* Rank. *Produced by* Steven Pallos *and* Pierre Braunberger. *Directed by* Dick Clement. *Written by* Dick Clement *and* Ian La Frenais, *based on the novel by* George Marton *and* Tibor Meray. *Photographed in Panavision and Technicolor by* Christopher Challis. *Edited by* John Bloom. *Art director,* Carmen Dillon. *Musical score by* Claude Bolling. *Running time:* 94 minutes.

CAST: Kirk Douglas *(Andrej),* Marlène Jobert *(Fabienne),* Trevor Howard *(Sir Trevor Dawson),* Tom Courtenay *(Baxter Clarke),* Patrick Mower *(John Fenton),* Bernadette Lafont *(Simone),* Bernard Blier *(Webb),* Sacha Pitoeff *(Stefan),* Richard Pearson *(Haldane),* Garfield Morgan *(Jealous Husband),* Angharad Rees *(Victoria),* Isabel Dean *(Celia),* Robin Parkinson *(British Officer),* Jonathan Cecil *(British Attaché),* Robert Raglan *(Ambassador).*

Although released in Europe late in 1971, *Catch Me a Spy* had not been seen in the United States at the time of completing this book—April of 1972. The film critics in London gave the film only faint praise, the consensus being that it was a moderately entertaining but not outstanding entry in the genre of slick espionage thrillers. Favorable comments were passed on it being neatly done, with an ingenious plot and an attractive cast, but that it lacked proper pacing and style. Mention was also made of its interesting use of various geographical locations, especially the photography of the scenes done in Scotland. In reviewing the film for Britain's *Monthly Film Bulletin,* Nigel Andrews concluded his critique: "Things pick up briefly toward the end, with some cat-and-mouse scenes in a deserted Scottish hotel, and there are enjoyable performances from Kirk Douglas and Marlène Jobert. But on the whole it's one of those films that were obviously more fun to make than they are to watch."

In *Catch Me a Spy* Kirk Douglas appears as a spy, but not one who gets caught. He is a Roumanian named Andrej and supposedly a waiter. The story revolves around a French girl living in London, Fabi-

With Marlene Jobert

enne (Marlène Jobert). She marries a young Englishman, John Fenton (Patrick Mower), who is, unknown to her, an agent in the employ of the Soviets. On their honeymoon in Bucharest he is arrested by the secret police, although the arrest is merely a ruse to contact him. Later the same day, a waiter in the hotel in which they are staying enters their room and conceals something in a suitcase. When Fabienne learns that her husband has been whisked off to Moscow, she returns to England and goes to seek the advice of her uncle, Sir Trevor Dawson (Trevor Howard), who happens to be a foreign office diplomat. He tells her John is being held by the Russians on a charge of espionage and that they are willing to exchange him for a Russian spy being held by the British. The deal falls through when the Russian spy is accidentally killed, and then Fabienne sets out to find some other spy to use as a barter. Eventually she settles on Andrej, who is now in London and trying to locate whatever it was he secreted in her suitcase.

Fabienne's attempts to trap Andrej come to no avail but one evening while they are together in her apartment, they are set upon and rendered unconscious by some mysterious assailants. When they awake they find they are in the back seat of a moving car; at an opportune moment they jump out and make their escape—and discover themselves to be in Scotland. They take refuge in a deserted hotel, where Andrej confesses to Fabienne that he is himself a spy and that his mission was to smuggle Russian documents out of Rumania and into England. He tells her one of his most important pieces of information is

contained on a microfilm in her suitcase. Fabienne finds herself drawn to Andrej, and she is horrified when he is later arrested in London and set up as the pawn to trade with the Russians in exchange for her husband. The scene of the exchange is a river at an Iron Curtain point. Andrej and Fabienne are on one

With Marlene Jobert

spy—Andrej, and we are left to assume she will be happy with him.

Catch Me a Spy was the third film in a row in which Kirk Douglas was actively involved in the production and the raising of financing. This is an involvement that is likely to continue as his career progresses. Douglas has never been content to be only an actor, and certainly not an actor at the mercy of the film industry and its frightening vicissitudes. The formation of his own company, Bryna, in 1955 was brought about not so much for reasons of ego but as a purely hard-headed business venture, "The impact of television brought enormous changes in the Hollywood studios, with fewer and fewer films being produced. Many stars found themselves unemployed and I wasn't about to let it happen to me. Some of us formed our own companies, Burt Lancaster and John Wayne are among the best examples, and we made our own deals with the studios. It was a matter of survival. It still is. I also feel that if we are to survive as film makers we are going to have to be more and more international. The more we cross frontiers to make co-productions and multi-national financing the better it will be for the future of this industry. Film financing, like gold, is where you find it. Today we are interinvolved and interdependent, and the future is bound to see an increase in these trends. This is a healthy development. If you assemble a cast which has stars drawn from different countries, you have built-in appeal for those countries when it comes to selling and distributing. Also, it's good that technicians of different countries work together. Film making is an international means of expression."

launch and John Fenton on another; as the boats draw up alongside, Andrej challenges John to open his suitcase, which he recognizes as the one in which he secreted the microfilm. John reluctantly opens the case and reveals it to be full of money—Andrej then grabs it and the panic stricken Englishman beats a hasty retreat, a retreat that costs him his bride, the microfilm and the money. Fabienne at last catches a

As this book was being written, Douglas was in Europe, making *A Man to Respect,* his own production, on location in Rome and Hamburg

A letter from **KIRK DOUGLAS** to the author

I've just received a wire asking me, urgently, to send you my feelings about the future of movies and my own future. It's rather appropriate that the wire reached me in Starigrad, a tiny town along the Adriatic in Yugoslavia. Here I'm preparing to direct a movie called *Scalawag*—my first film as a director. Of course, I've been *accused* of directing movies before but now I can be blamed.

So I suppose that tells you my present as well as my future. I want to keep on making movies. Hopefully, I will direct more than act, although I'm also acting in *Scalawag.* After all, how many actors can I get to be directed by me the first time?

I want to make a real *movie.* I don't want to be profound or intellectual, or sway someone to my way of thinking. I want my film to contain all the nostalgic elements that used to thrill me years ago—pirates, cowboys, treasures, killing but no blood, death but no dying. I just want to make a movie to help people forget their own problems and to get lost in the problems of the people on the screen. Isn't that what going to the movies is all about?

And if I succeed, I'll go on making movies. And if I don't, I'll be an ex-movie maker.

KIRK DOUGLAS

May 17, 1972
Starigrad, Yugoslavia.

Douglas with his wife in Hamburg, during the filming
of *A Man to Respect*